HERITAGE FROM HAMILTON

Painted by Walter Robertson. Engraved by George Graham. For James, Rivington New-York.

Heritage from Hamilton

By BROADUS MITCHELL

1957

COLUMBIA UNIVERSITY PRESS, NEW YORK

© 1957

COLUMBIA UNIVERSITY PRESS, NEW YORK

PUBLISHED IN

GREAT BRITAIN, CANADA,

INDIA, AND PAKISTAN

BY THE OXFORD UNIVERSITY PRESS

LONDON, TORONTO,

BOMBAY, AND KARACHI

MANUFACTURED IN THE

UNITED STATES OF AMERICA

LIBRARY OF CONGRESS CATALOG

CARD NUMBER: 57-12572

The portrait on the title page is taken from an engraving by George Graham from a painting by Walter Robertson. It was made for James Rivington, who sold many portrait prints of public figures. Camillus was the pseudonym used by Hamilton in controversy over the Jay Treaty (1795), but the uniform, that of the Inspector-General, he would have worn in 1798.

IN MEMORIAM

SAMUEL CHILES MITCHELL

1864–1948

FOREWORD

𝒯HE opportunity to offer the Gino Speranza Lectures in Columbia University is a distinction. For the academic year 1956–57 it is a particular privilege. This is because of the suggestion that the place of Alexander Hamilton in American traditions and ideals be the chosen topic. Hamilton was educated at King's College, 1773–76, and received an honorary degree in 1788 from its successor, Columbia College, which he served as Trustee. The present year, under auspices of a national commission of which the President of the United States is honorary chairman, is being celebrated as the bicentennial of Hamilton's birth. This all but corresponds with the bicentennial of Columbia also.

While many occasions, commencing in the United States Congress and spreading to all parts of the country, are recalling Hamilton's contribution, none can express the same pride as the participation of Columbia University. For his career shows the blessing—one may almost say the indispensable quality—of liberal education turned to the uses of public life. If Columbia had conferred this training on no other among scores of thousands, the costs and pains of this institution would have made a grateful return to America. Besides the impetus which Hamilton imparted to the national economy and polity, he more specifically paid tribute to his education here by enlarging in the legislature the scope of the Board of Regents of New York, and gave his name to another college of the state which shares special esteem for him.

Much of Hamilton's work, official and professional, required the highest technical proficiency, but he received none of that in the classroom. Today's solicitude for specialized training, particularly in the physical sciences and engineering, necessary as changed circumstances demand it, should not obscure the claim of broad acquaintance with the life of man, social, mental, moral, and aesthetic, which we call liberal education. This, if anything, may improve perspective for our country and the whole human family, and in the same breath inspire the wish to forward joy and dignity in our common concerns. On this firm footing may be erected, by less difficult means, the superstructure of scientific inquiry and serviceable application.

Alexander Hamilton was born with genius. But here he knocked on the generous door which opened to his fame and his country's benefit. The direction of his faculties, here more than elsewhere, bore the results which the following pages seek to estimate.

BROADUS MITCHELL

New York, New York
April, 1957

CONTENTS

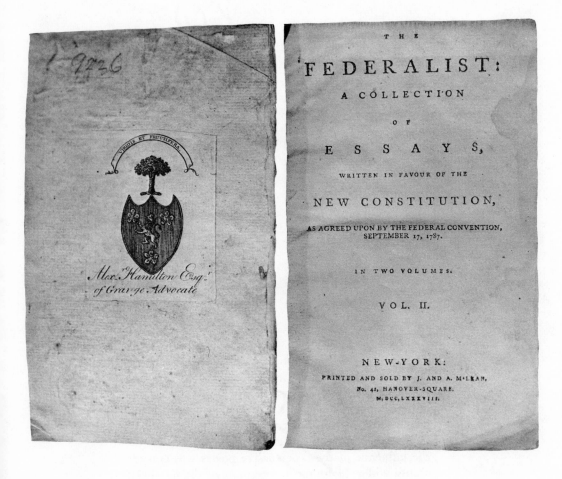

THE

FEDERALIST:

A COLLECTION

OF

ESSAYS,

WRITTEN IN FAVOUR OF THE

NEW CONSTITUTION,

AS AGREED UPON BY THE FEDERAL CONVENTION,
SEPTEMBER 17, 1787.

IN TWO VOLUMES.

VOL. II.

NEW-YORK:

PRINTED AND SOLD BY J. AND A. M'LEAN,
No. 41, HANOVER-SQUARE.
M,DCC,LXXXVIII.

Title page of first edition of *The Federalist* (Hamilton's personal copy, in the possession of Columbia University). These essays began appearing in newspapers soon after the text of the Constitution was offered to the country. Originally designed to secure ratification by the critical state of New York, the influence of these persuasive pieces was considerably wider. Hamilton wrote most of the numbers, Madison half as many, and Jay a few. *The Federalist* is the most celebrated commentary on the American Constitutional system.

$\mathcal{I}_N$ this summary treatment, in comment on Hamilton's beginnings, we are tempted to take too long a run for our leap. And yet the little known first third of his life, in the West Indies, held features powerful in his later career. It is a dramatic reflection that this child, who was to comprehend the promise of an imperial continent, was born, to the best of our belief, on the merest speck of an island in the blue Caribbean, miles from our mainland and 1,300 miles from New York. Nevis is a volcanic cone, only five miles in diameter at the gently sloping shores. Its lofty crater, no longer belching brimstone, is generally enveloped in its own clinging, snowy cloud. The modest settlement of Charles Town, behind the western crescent beach, is unchanged in two hundred years, except that the stone fort and some of the houses, hardly less somber and substantial, have yielded to hurricane or neglect. On the front street is the reputed birthplace of our hero. The double flight of steps gives entrance to vacancy, and the garden wall encloses only weeds. This is the empty shell in the silent nest.

It would be quite possible for a parson or storekeeper, in Hamilton's childhood or since, to know every man, woman, child, donkey, and goat on the island. Its minute life, vastly detached from all but the neighboring St. Kitts, made Nevis, for these very reasons, a fortunate point of origin for one who was to help create American dominion. He came to the Continent a visitor, without roots in any part of it, and hence could adopt all of it.

Also this boy, whose passion was to be organization, came from a completely broken home and kindred. Born out of wedlock, he was left an orphan at thirteen by the death of his mother, following the earlier permanent departure of his father on island wanderings. By this time, doubtless through several transfers which we cannot trace, Alexander had been taken from British Nevis to Danish St. Croix (Christiansted). Here his mother's relatives, formerly notably prosperous, suddenly disintegrated in estate, physical and moral, at just the time when he was most in need of their rescue. Causes are unimportant for us; they embraced sale of the uncle's home plantation to an incompetent debtor, the absconding of one cousin, suicide of another, and a succession of disappointing marriages by a third. This last, however, though clutching at remnants, was the only one of the clan in fact eager to share with Alexander.

This explosion of fortunes put a cap to earlier mischiefs in his family history. His mother, Rachael Faucette (anglicized from the French form to Fawcett) before his birth had been imprisoned by her husband on scandalous charges which ended in his divorcing her. The court forbade her to remarry. In a few years, still young and spirited, her affections were for the first time engaged, by a Scotsman, James Hamilton, offshoot of an ancient house in Ayrshire. Among his endearing qualities, ability to make a living for his common-law wife and two sons, James, the elder, and Alexander, was not numbered. Still, somehow they rubbed along, defying convention with mutual affection for a decade before he passed, to all intents, from the picture. Rachael, with a small inheritance from her mother, bravely made the best of a hard lot by opening a little store in the principal town of St. Croix, where the boys may have helped her measure out homely staple provisions. This for a few years until she died of a fever, and her sons, in heavy veils, watched her body interred in a grave long lost to memory.

Incidentally, in the aftermath of inventory of her pathetic effects, it came out, before the probate judge, that Alexander was born, if we may believe the evidence, two years earlier than has hitherto been supposed, that is, in 1755 instead of 1757. We have some corroborative testimony in his own chary allusions to his history. If true, his precociousness is turned only from the astonishing to the credible; it helps us to understand his early maturity, as aide to Washington at twenty-two, not twenty, and his appointment to the United States Treasury at thirty-four, not thirty-two.

Several biographers have inevitably been busy with the readymade certainty that Alexander Hamilton had his happy combination of traits from the quick French blood of his mother and the calculating Caledonian derivation of his father. Animation and perception were surely joined in him with the prudent habit of second thoughts, but attributing this blend of endowments to racial strains seems conjectural.

In any case, with verve and system, he promptly overcame obstacles. Perhaps his zeal was spurred beyond the ordinary by the lapses of his relatives. His performance as clerk, at desk and counter, in the trading post of Nicholas Cruger in St. Croix led to a new prospect. And well it might, for what other teenager showed such eager discharge of responsibilities beyond his years? We have a sheaf of his business letters written in a period of months as proxy for his absent employer. They show grown-up judgment added to youthful exultant energy. This experience of import-export traffic by the little sloops of the time, shuttling to Boston, New York, Philadelphia, and the Spanish Main, informed him on the economy of the island of St. Croix. The main export was muscovado sugar; most provisions and all manufactures must be brought in from Denmark or the Continent. Thus the society was a dependent one with the inevitable hazards of staple agriculture. The basis of all was sun and slavery. A small minority of elegant planters, and the merchants, ship captains, officials, and soldiers who did their bidding, ground the black work force overwhelmingly outnumbering all whites. The severity of labor and cruelties of discipline shock the modern reader of abundant records. Driven to desperation but unable to escape the island, slaves recurrently revolted, burning canefields, murdering overseers and masters. Torpor of the economy was matched by terror of the mind.

These effects could not have escaped Alexander's reflection. If afterward, in a new setting and called to act a public part, he made himself the engine of a varied, balanced economy, and the constant foe of slavery, he was improving lessons learned in the predatory paradise of his youth.

From St. Croix, at seventeen, by pluck and luck Alexander was whisked to New York for an education. Cruger, admiring and generous, was a younger son of a great New York merchant family. His partner, Cornelius Kortright, was another. Alexander's cousin Ann (née Lytton) lent what she could wangle from her inheritance. What sparked this cooperation of his friends was doubtless the pleas of Hugh Knox, Presbyterian clergyman and perceptive patron. Native of northern Ireland, teacher in Delaware, graduate of Princeton, for twenty years his spirit had survived island isolation. Newly arrived on St. Croix, he discovered Alexander, fed his mind, and espoused his ambition. Here Knox found the complete little man of business, who yet devoured books, wrote verses (sacred and profane) for the local newspaper, absorbed sermons and more potent private exhortations. The pupil's faculties were confined only by his narrow opportunities. His avidity reached to the cynical monitions of Machiavelli, not offset by the couplets of Pope or the classic histories of Plutarch. He pondered and praised the British constitution. Shouldn't there be something for this surprising youngster beyond the mongering of molasses and salt cod, mules and human workstock?

The story, maybe authentic because first printed by Hamilton's son, is that, in the words of Mrs. Atherton's biographical novel *The Conqueror*, a hurricane of August, 1772, "blew him into history." Warmed by Knox's public sermon, Alexander described the wreck of the island in a letter to his father. The preacher showed it around for its florid picture and piety. Over Alexander's protest, Knox inserted it in the island newspaper. Whether or not, the catastrophe arousing charity, this letter turned the trick, Alexander's friends rallied and dispatched him to the Continent with the promise of consignments of sugar to defray his schooling.

He landed at Boston, perhaps in the autumn of 1772, where Sam Adams was damning Parliament and Hancock was parading the city militia. But the young visitor's preference for British authority did not yield then nor for some months afterward. He posted to New York, bearing letters from Knox to Presbyterian worthies, and was received by Cruger's merchant correspondents, Kortright & Co. (It chanced, by the by, that Kortright land embraced the site of the present Columbia University.) In preparation for college, Alexander was handed over to the tutelage of Francis Barber at his academy at Elizabethtown, New Jersey, where he seems to have spent the better part of a year under the patronage of William Livingston and Elias Boudinot and part of the time lived in the effulgent home of the latter. Swiftly repairing his deficiencies in the classics, and by now won to republican hopes, Alexander was presented to President Witherspoon with every academic and sectarian entitlement for admission. He preferred Princeton because it was politically more dissentient than loyal King's College in New York. After oral quiz, Witherspoon highly approved him, but the rules, it turned out, could not be bent to Alexander's insistence that he be allowed to pass through the courses as rapidly as he could dispatch them, without regard to class years. Thence perforce to King's, where aristocratic leniency made exception in his case, setting an example of discretion which registrars, beset as they doubtless are, may well remember.

So New York became his home for life. Hamilton's Continental outlook, predisposed by his arrival from a distant island, could not have been preserved so faithfully through crowded years of legislature, Congress, conventions, and cabinet had fortune cast his lot elsewhere. Had he remained in Boston he would not have found himself at the hub of the American universe. New England was earlier fervid in the colonies' cause than New York, and continued Federalist longer, but with all its influence it was at a geographic extreme. The West Indies had contacts with the Carolinas; Knox's brother was at Edenton and Alexander's half-brother was making a tidy fortune near Charleston. But that was at the other end of the country and would have identified our hero with the fiercest localism of all. To Virginia he had no introduction, but with all

the Old Dominion's national contribution, later political developments, had he located there, would have put him at a sectional disadvantage as a Continental advocate. Good men grew in New
Jersey, those who befriended Alexander Hamilton foremost among
them, but the short sail from Elizabethtown Point to the Battery
was, for Hamilton's future, a transfer of immense consequence.

As New Yorker, Hamilton was in mid-position. Increasingly,
from harbor and hinterland, New York city drew economic resources which recommended its political counsel. Hamilton the
better used this fulcrum to pry other parts into national compliance
because his pride in New York never made him, like George Clinton, its proprietary champion. His marriage, while yet in the army,
to Elizabeth, daughter of General Philip Schuyler of Albany, aided
and abetted his Continental viewpoint and urgings, for Schuyler's
penchant was all of that sort, and each gave to the other's enthusiasm and designs. Further, embraced in trust and affection into the
Schuyler family and following, Hamilton had an upstate as well
as southern counties influence, without which his Federalist pretensions would have been dishonored at home.

In reaction to pro-British preceptors at King's, especially President Myles Cooper and his Anglican supporters, the young col-
legian began contributing to the patriot newspaper of John Holt.
For the likely identification of these anonymous pieces we have
much to hope from researches of the editors of a comprehensive
collection of Hamilton's writings, now in progress in Columbia
University.

These pieces in the press led on to his impetuous speech at the
meeting in the Fields (now City Hall Park) in July, 1774, in support of democratically chosen delegates to the Continental Congress. This was his first public identification with resistance. More
deliberate were his two long pamphlets answering the Tory "West-
chester Farmer," the doughty Samuel Seabury. While the apologist
of Parliament had addressed himself to New Yorkers, our col-
legian's replies embraced all of the colonies. He had come to know

McDougall, Lamb, Sears, Willett, and others of the Liberty Boys who were not squeamish about a little mob violence. Hamilton would have none of this. He protested when Rivington's types were destroyed, and saved President Cooper from a coat of tar and feathers by hastening him over the back fence of the College when his would-be punishers had broken down the gate. Hamilton harangued the ugly crowd, and later, with characteristic thoroughness, he joined Cooper, wandering on the river bank, and escorted him to a place of refuge.

By stages of student drill, and then membership in the militia, Hamilton left college in the spring of 1776 when he obtained the captaincy of the New York Artillery Company. Before the Battle of Long Island this was mustered into Continental service, shared Washington's retreat to Pennsylvania, blasted away at the British in the surprise attacks on Trenton and Princeton, and wound up in winter quarters at Morristown. Soon (March 1, 1777) he was appointed one of the aides of the commander in chief, with the rank of lieutenant colonel. We may choose between several stories, all honorific, of how Alexander Hamilton came to the notice of Washington. He had refused staff invitations from two general officers earlier, preferring field command. Though later, momentarily, he regretted leaving the line for the headquarters "military family," his service of four years (nearly the longest of all of the aides) in closest association with Washington probably determined his after career. He was hourly with the commander in chief in battle, bivouac, and camp—dispatching orders, preparing reports, and corresponding, under Washington's direction, with Congress and all commanders. He became Washington's other self, which could not have been without a deal of originality in the young aide. In this confidential association Hamilton knew the whole problem of Revolutionary America, military, political, economic. His deep concern prompted him to his own proposals to Robert Morris and others for solution, without in any way committing Washington. A tiff with Washington, when nerves of both were frayed, was

quickly followed by renewed understanding between them and en-
trusting of Colonel Hamilton with capture of the last British redoubt at Yorktown.

Notable figures who served during the Revolution in legislature,
executive office, and diplomatic assignment complained that the
Society of the Cincinnati set up a presumed preference of patriotism
for those in the army. No moral distinction was implied by the
Cincinnati and yet, in the sequel of political developments, ex-
officers of the army had a genuine advantage. Veterans, in the eyes
of the country, have been clothed with special gratitude, though
sometimes they have been treated to empty praise and pity. Chief
army officers had acquired intimate knowledge of each other under
trying circumstances. They had acted together for the whole
country, many of them in every theater of the war. They shared
a personal attachment to Washington which translated itself into
national action as civilians. This common experience by no means
barred political differences, but the bond was material, particularly
in the formative stages of establishing the independent government.
Further, army men saw the weaknesses of wartime government
from the most critical angle, and they were ready to condemn the
same symptoms after the peace. Many of them, therefore, like
Hamilton, in putting off the tunic felt a special call to don the
toga.

Hamilton, at Washington's headquarters, had been at the opera-
tive center of the national struggle. He had come to know and
could estimate principal men from all parts of the country. His
service as aide to Washington had been as much political and
diplomatic as military, though the commander in chief deferred
perhaps too scrupulously to the civil authority. Hamilton early saw
that to win the war, government must be drawn to a focus and
economic resources must be marshaled. His later work was an extension of these earlier, partial, disappointed pleas. His lengthy
arguments to Duane and Morris, begging for responsible administration and a publicly sponsored bank, in the course of a decade took
on sharper definition, but they remained the same in scope and

purpose. All was for strengthening the central authority, *de facto*, in what could not yet be a nation in the sense of political organization. Others were disgusted with Congress and alarmed by disorder in the finances, but nobody else, at least in the army, analyzed with such vigor or formulated remedies with such documentation.

Like Tom Paine, Hamilton wrote on a drum-head. However, Paine's patriotic exhortation, the most moving of its kind, did not involve the distraction of devising institutional remedies. Hamilton reviewed history, invoked the experience of other countries, cited figures, drew up detailed instruments. A clue to his means is in the last paybook of his New York Artillery Company. His command was handed over when he joined Washington's staff, and the book remained with him as a receipt; he used blank pages at the back for notes of his reading in Postlethwayt's *Dictionary* and other compendia. Similar memoranda of the war years exist, though probably more have been lost except as they appeared in his advocacies. How he found time for economic logistics we may only guess. We know from his whole life that his industry and faculty of concentration were phenomenal. He turned from one task to another in rapid succession and executed each with thoroughness and finish. Distinguished contemporaries were obliged to clear away and square off for a new project. They waited for favorable intervals. Hamilton kept several undertakings in the works at once. Hamilton College treasures his camp writing desk, a speaking memorial of the many kinds of papers he prepared. Later others collaborated with him in objects that taxed overtime effort, notably Madison and Jay in *The Federalist*. But their contributions were fewer and had the benefit of more leisure. In spite of a demanding law practice, in a prodigious spurt he supplied eighteen numbers of this series in a block.

After Yorktown he repaired to Albany for what was almost his only period of absorption in a single object, brief study for admission to the bar. For once he had to ask for a short extension of time, for the examination. But even so he rocked his son's cradle while mastering basic texts and manuals and, as a by-product, made his own handbook of practice in the Supreme Court of New York. A copy of this, one of several known to have been made by other students and young practitioners, has recently turned up, and testifies to his penchant for reducing vexing detail to system. He was still walking the floor with Blackstone and the baby when he yielded to the repeated plea of the Superintendent of Finance that he become Receiver of Continental Revenue for New York, in the summer of 1782. This sounds passive. In fact, he had to devise a tax system for his state if proceeds were to flow to the central treasury. He must meet with committees of the legislature to inform and persuade, must make himself mustermaster for whatever resources could be wrung for the nation from reluctant governor and counties not still occupied by the enemy. He was not only Morris's energetic local lieutenant, but cooperated in his chief's plans for the country's currency and credit. His work was preparatory. This apprenticeship helped to place him in the United States Treasury seven years later, for it was introduction to the practice of public finance and earned him the recommendation of Robert Morris. He relinquished his post because the legislature, admiring his zeal (though not responding with funds), elected him to Congress.

Here commenced a new phase of Hamilton's service to the country. It was a parlous period in which, pending the treaties of peace, economic and political wreckage of the war was to undergo emergency repair. More foreign loans could be wheedled only if supported by establishment of unquestioned revenue under the sole control of Congress. Hamilton threw his whole force into improving and pressing the proposal of a federal import duty collected by loyal agents. Every objection was raised, every footless delay was devised, every exasperating reversal of consent was practiced by inhibited colleagues reflecting the exhaustion and jealousies in their states. When at length all seemed in train except recalcitrant Rhode Island, and Hamilton had prepared a last remonstrance and persuasion to Newport, Virginia backslid and his own New York attached unacceptable conditions to compliance. This was in the

face of a clamorous army at Newburgh which could not be disbanded—if indeed that was militarily safe—without being paid.
Hamilton was desperate. While, on the one hand, he joined with
his father-in-law, Schuyler, in a noble call, adopted by the New
York legislature, for a constitutional convention to enable a new
start, he briefly toyed with the notion that aggrieved soldiers might
collect their arrears at bayonet-point and also assist to recruit the
general credit. He promptly dropped this dangerous idea and aided
Washington in reproving incipient rebellion of officers in the en-
campment.

The incident, happily got over, requires a pause. Certain critics
have ventured that Hamilton, in his vehement nationalism, was ever
impatient with constitutional limitations and, had opportunity offered in the course of developments, would have become, in modern
terms, fascist. They have supported this contention by pointing to
his later furious disappointment when the provisional army, of
which he was chief organizer, was dissolved because President
Adams, after warlike threats, composed differences with France.
The allegation is that Hamilton had reached the stage of wanting
to subvert political government and employ large armed forces
under his command for domination at home and conquest abroad,
à la Napoleon. We shall come to that question in course. Here we
must note that his indulgence in the conjecture of military rule, or
extempore military assistance to civil authority, in 1783, though
swiftly put by, betrays a contrast to the steady wisdom of Washington. Washington, too, more than a decade later, not a little abetted
by Hamilton, was eager to discountenance dissenting political societies and to punish their leaders, especially if believed to be under foreign influence. But, without doubt, Washington's political prudence
and patience were superior to Hamilton's. In their collaboration of
many years Hamilton was the quicker and more fertile in expedients and of unexampled service in executing agreed policy. But
his direction-needle did not point to the lodestar as unwaveringly
as did Washington's. The temperamental and moral difference
argues a defect in Hamilton, though all additional acquaintance

with the period confirms the popular conviction, then and since, that Washington set a standard not matched by any of his contemporaries.

Hardly was the Newburgh crisis overcome when Hamilton played a chief part, as spokesman of Congress, in suppressing mutinous troops who menaced its meetings. Further, he characteristically protested against the failure of the Pennsylvania authorities to support the safety and dignity of the national body. As chairman of a committee he reported to President Boudinot that Congress should be moved to the rural protection of Princeton. This incident helped produce the demand for a federal district over which Congress could exercise complete sway, and the eventual choice of location, as we shall see, became a bargaining point in adoption of Hamilton's fiscal system.

He lingered in Congress during the summer of 1783 vainly hoping the preliminary treaty of peace would arrive, but finally put out for New York to establish his home and law office (in Wall Street). He found the city in no peaceful mood. Already, in advance of evacuation, British merchants were fleeing from threats of vindictive patriots. Right at the start Hamilton protested against the rashness of depriving the community of men of capital and enterprise who would be sorely needed in reconstructing the economy. In the coming months he broadened his appeal for fair treatment of Tories and their sympathizers. He published his *Phocion* articles, begging that former enemies, where they wished to remain as useful citizens or residents, should be protected in their civil and property rights. As a practical matter, why drive off competent persons to strengthen Canada, likely to become a competitor or even a foe? His sensible arguments might well have been reverted to when we deported enemy aliens and other suspected residents after World War I. They apply with greater force to the recent, or current, frenzy for denying civil liberties in the name of national security. Later, when he had chief responsibility for girding for war with France, he too far consented in the Alien and Sedition

Acts, which makes it the more suitable to dwell on his advice when he was calmer.

Hamilton's remonstrances were without effect. The legislature was zestful, under Governor George Clinton's command, to banish and expropriate. War measures to these ends of punishing former enemies, foreign and domestic, were confirmed and extended in rapid succession. The notorious Trespass Act gave patriots the right to sue for recovery of the rents of their property enjoyed by the British during the occupation. This, Hamilton declared, was an infraction of the treaty of peace which was the supreme law of the land. No state, under whatever provocation, could defy this national engagement. Our new independence must not be smirched with dishonor. He did put a check to this rampage by winning the most celebrated of his early law cases, in which he appeared for the defendant Waddington against the Widow Rutgers.

Waddington, a British merchant, had used a brewhouse and some other property of Mrs. Rutgers under authority of the military commander of the city to whom he paid his rent. Braving almost unanimous public hostility, Hamilton secured a judgment from the mayor's court (from which there was no legal appeal) freeing Waddington of liability under the charge of trespass. The state law, Hamilton maintained, however explicit, was null and void in face of the treaty which was national sovereignty. Organized city protest demanded that the legislature displace the members of the court, but in vain. After this success, Hamilton was flooded with other cases of similar sort, and the professional harvest he now reaped was an early count in the accusation which followed him in one way and another during the remainder of the life, namely, that he was pro-British. The passionate, goaded by the inescapable injuries of war, failed to see that he was truly pro-American, for the sake of legal integrity, political comity, and economic advancement of his young country.

The shortcomings of the Confederation were as inevitable as they were unmistakable. A hastily summoned meeting of delegates from

the colonies grew, by emergency consent, into the central govern-
ing body during a protracted war. Its most essential work was
done without benefit of a constitution. The finances were bound to
be left in disarray. While interest accrued alarmingly, the morale
of Congress and country sank to complaisance in the prospect of
repudiation of the domestic debt. Distant from one another by
crude means of travel, the states were divergent politically and
economically. Untaught by after-events, each clutched its own
sovereignty. The war aim continued to invest most minds, not
knowing that independence is less than freedom. Indulging jealousy,
the states could not rise to joint effort. Time was the cure, and
the wonder is that it was so foreshortened. The blessing was a
British political heritage. Recently an American visitor who had
struggled to grow decent grass around her new suburban home was
admiring the sward of one of the Oxford colleges. "How do you
get this golf-green perfection?" she asked the gardener. "That's
easy," he explained. "You cut, and sprinkle, and roll, and fertilize,
and cut and roll and water again. You do this for seven hundred
years and you have a lawn like this." The lesson makes for patience
with countries while they are trying to raise themselves to competence in a twinkling.

In judging of the Confederation, extenuation is more suitable
than defense. Marshal counterclaim as ingeniously as you will, John
Fiske was right. The performance from Yorktown to the Constitution was abominable, and alert men of the time knew it. Obstacles
to internal and external trade paralyzed the first step toward improvement. Competitive tariffs impoverished all and exacerbated
political quarrels. Forebearing to rehearse tragicomic illustrations,
it is pleasanter to praise James Madison for his early moves to
ameliorate the evils as between Virginia and Maryland. Washington, equally eager, wanted to construct navigation to the interior.
From their efforts, by stages, came the Annapolis Commercial Convention in 1786. This is one of the notable historical instances in
which failure produced unexpected success. It is almost an argument for irresponsible neglect. Delegates of some states, duly ap-

pointed, never set out. Others never arrived. Maryland, the host, sent none. Men from Virginia, Pennsylvania, New Jersey, Delaware, and New York waited impotently for more to come. We may guess at sober reflections in their informal conversations as they cooled their heels. When at length, despairing of their fellows, they sat down in session, all realized that too few states were present to serve the commercial objects. Abraham Clark of New Jersey, which had given her delegates latitude, got quick response when he blurted that the footless meeting should demand political renovation for America.

He must have taken the words out of the mouth of Alexander Hamilton, who drafted the call for a national constitutional convention to assemble the following year in Philadelphia. We are told that the hesitant Governor Edmund Randolph of Virginia reduced the vehemence of the indictment of the Confederation. Hamilton's original paper is lost, maybe burned up by the words he wrote on it. In any event the country rose to his argument and plea, however revised, in sudden common consent. Hamilton's conviction that economic betterment waited on political reorganization was not singular to him, but he held and preached it with peculiar force. The country needed concert and plan; the central authority must be able to regulate interstate and foreign commerce and command national revenue. Sovereignty was a condition precedent to solvency.

This was the mercantilist idea, without reference to particular mercantilist measures. Hamilton promoted its adoption in America some decades after Europe had begun to depreciate the role of government, making private capitalist enterprise the cynosure. Adam Smith's *Wealth of Nations* had been published a decade before, and earlier the French physiocrats had celebrated the wisdom of let-alone. It must be remembered that America was undeveloped, with slender resources in individual hands. Here association, not autonomy of effort, was appropriate. Decision, initiative must be collective before individual, and national before local. The revolt against mercantilism, or against British colonialism, though it accomplished our independence, was premature in the New World. After a brief fling with the minimum of national control we were obliged to "consolidate" our system, put the states in second place, and give central government powers over citizens immediately. Shays's Rebellion in Massachusetts was more than a passing disturbance that persuaded the constitutional fathers to forbid any state to pass laws violating the obligation of contracts. It was a blow to the pretension of the member state to self-sufficiency in a loose confederation. The state did not, could not, preserve order, protect life and property.

As he had been the voice of the Annapolis meeting, if nothing more, Hamilton was naturally chosen by the New York legislature as a delegate to the Constitutional Convention. But Governor Clinton thought to overbalance him by sending along two state's rights dependables, Robert Yates and John Lansing, Jr. As long as they were present they determined the vote of New York against Hamilton's contentions for a vigorous national government. Steadily at odds with his own colleagues, his credit was diminished in the eyes of the convention. Fortunately, like Luther Martin of Maryland, convinced that the importance of the states was being sacrificed, Yates and Lansing quit in disgust, thus marching themselves off the page of history. Hamilton was thereafter freer, though New York, with him as single representative, had no vote.

His principal deliverance was in the middle of June, when the Virginia (Madison-Randolph) and New Jersey (Paterson) plans had been offered. The first, enlarging and stiffening the central powers, became the basis of the Constitution as adopted. The second, little improvement over the Articles of Confederation, did not detain the delegates long, but its inhibitions made Hamilton's proposals the more striking, indeed shocking. Hitherto silent, he spoke for the whole day, developing a compact outline of which we have the text. He was not offering a plan which he believed could be approved; he threw in his views for discussion, to test the length to which others would go, and to nudge opinions closer to his ideal of an effective national system. A limited monarchy, like the British, was the best form for such an extensive country as ours, but this he would not urge because America was wedded to republican principles.

As the next best expedient, Hamilton proposed a chief executive chosen practically for life, holding the balance between the excitable body of the people on the one hand, and the minority of citizens of property and position on the other. The democratic lower house was to be elected directly by the people for a short term; the senators, named by electors chosen by the people, should serve for life. The states, except as convenient administrative units, ought to be erased, but short of this, the way to extinguish their separate sovereignties was to give the President appointment of the governors, who must have absolute veto on all local laws. The acts of Congress were to be supreme in the land, but with the right of a powerful federal judiciary to declare any national law unconstitutional.

All hearers praised the fire and conviction of his declaration, but none agreed with him. Maybe his bold proposition was the wisest means of influencing the convention. There was no doubt of his candor. Leading features of his scheme had received partial approval earlier, for example, a President for life. Farthest to the right, he took the curse from the approaches of others. If perverse, he was provocative. Nor did he, later in the sessions, isolate himself by proving dogmatic and stubborn. On the contrary, having beckoned toward a government competent to the crisis, he was indefatigable in composing differences on the floor and in fashioning the best instrument that could be obtained. His detailed constitution, written out later in the sittings when he had been taught by the drift of debate, modified his original conceptions. His efforts, on a visit to New Jersey and New York, for a feasible conclusion to the labors of the convention were valued by Washington. Hamilton alone, for New York, signed the final document, when members as diverse as Martin and Mason, Randolph and Gerry refused to put their names to it. His exertions, through the *Federalist* papers, for approval by the states and his heroic fight for ratification in New York are better known.

Viewing his part in the convention, how accurate is the popular belief that Hamilton scorned the discretion of the people and seized the opportunity, so far as in him lay, to construct a new government vesting power in property and privilege? Indeed, that this was the cunning aim of the convention as a whole is the celebrated proposition of the late Professor Charles A. Beard. Many persons consider that Hamilton was the extreme type of designing aristocrats who, in secret and unworthily, devised a fundamental law to rescue their threatened material claims. Beard's economic interpretation of the Constitution has enjoyed substantial credence for several reasons. Its announcement in 1913 roughly coincided with the arrival in the United States of socialism with its emphasis on class interests, as a familiar, though far from generally accepted, point of view on social development. More narrowly, the historical school of economists was commending itself in this country. Beard examined with pains the security holding and land speculations of members of the convention, treating these personages no longer as demigods but as men with human frailties like the rest of us. He named names, exposed private concerns of individuals, which, especially when applied to the famous, takes the eye. Reputations mounted in the firmament were brought to earth.

Perhaps Beard's was an over-correction of our historical astigmatism, so that we have been bent too much at the new angle. Our forefathers were not a different breed of men, but, called on to play a public part in the country's emergency, they summoned their full powers, which were mostly of marked good will. Similar circumstances of national need have produced similar results since, though not, as we see it, in quite that classic form. While it would be fatuous to suppose that material promptings were absent (for we know they were not), one may venture that moral motives were superior in their operation. Particular counter-arguments to

Beard's brilliant generalization need not detain us here.* As to Alexander Hamilton, unfortunately for the vulgar impression, Beard was obliged to number him among those who had no securities or land claims to burgeon under favorable central governmental authority. Hamilton's prospects were those of gratifying income from arduous practice of his profession of the law, from which now and later he distracted himself *pro bono publico*.

True, General Schuyler was wealthy, and Mrs. Hamilton as his daughter might expect one day to inherit a competence—which, in fact, however, did not happen. Hamilton, by taste, marriage, residence in a commercial city, and client connections was drawn to the side of aristocracy and conservatism in the conventional sense. Some, of psychological twist, have conjectured that this preference was compensation for the insecurity of his boyhood, just as they have supposed that his love of military glory would, in his own mind, add height to his slight five feet seven inches. Doubtless these influences figured insensibly. Some was accident, much was nature, more was reason. We must not confuse person and philosophy beyond a certain point. Hamilton was impressed with the necessity of repairs to the country consequent on colonial subordination, costs of war, and confusion in the aftermath of independence. His advocacies could not consist in abstractions, such as the rights of man. His principle of orderly progress in national strength immediately translated itself into concrete policies. These broke down to restored credit, reliable and abundant currency, and varied industry. Such achievements would not be induced by exhortation and would be imperiled by further delay. Therefore a national will must be enabled to reward and punish. This meant economic, social, and political control.

Where was this control to be vested? Surely in the national organs, for wrangling states, pulling and hauling for local advantage, had reduced the country to imbecility. His program de-

* See Robert E. Brown, *Charles Beard and the Constitution* (Princeton University Press, 1956).

manded for its execution restraint as well as boldness. The central
authority must claim "the regular weight . . . it will receive from
those who will find it their interest to support a government intended to preserve the peace and happiness of the community of
the whole." The segment of the population appropriately devoted
to maintaining stability and systematic advance was composed of
those of wealth and birth. "Give therefore to [this] class a distinct,
permanent share in the government. They will check the un-
steadiness," "the imprudence of democracy." But the elite and
fortunate were not to have sole sway. They were to hold office
by a "responsible" but "temporary or defeasible tenure." We must
not forget that to prevent oppression of the people, and denial of
individual liberties, the lower house by Hamilton's plan was to be
elected directly by the suffrage of all free males aged twenty-one
and upward—a more democratic provision than prevailed in most
of the states. This was an immediate counterpoise to the lifetime
senate which, in his original proposal, was to be chosen by electors
designated by all the voters. In his later scheme he provided that
those naming senatorial electors should have a certain property
qualification. The selection of the President was to be three removes
from the mass of the people. However, in Hamilton's revised plan,
the chief executive had a term of only three years.

We must take Hamilton in his time. He believed that over a
period the people, with benefit of a gryoscope to keep the ship
of state steady while they came to a deliberate conclusion on the
course, would determine right. It was in the short run that they
were turbulent and vulnerable to demagogic flattery. He was thus
far suspicious of the capacity of the people, at a given juncture, to
protect their own interests. Approval of pure democracy was far
more limited in America then than since. For convincing illustration, Thomas Jefferson felt that certain governmental officers
should be chosen by a prudentially restricted electorate.

So much for constitutional contrivance. The related, but more
insistent, question is whether wealth or commonwealth claimed

Hamilton's solicitude. The answer is plain in his whole life that he worked for the peace, prosperity, and freedom of the entire community. His client was not a class, but the country. He wanted to employ the privileged class for the general benefit, he did not allow himself to be used by this minority. Superficially dividing the dramatis personae of our early history into "good man" and "bad man," it has seemed to most, though with enthusiastic acknowledgment of his technical skill, that Hamilton belongs with the latter. It is difficult to refute this illusion while standing on one foot. Two signal circumstances may be mentioned. Handling millions for the public, he left the Treasury a poor man. Nearly at the end of his life, to prevent Burr, whom he distrusted as a self-serving potential dictator, from becoming president, he threw his whole influence to his inveterate political enemy, Jefferson. But acquaintance with his thought and actions, in all of the manifestations that we can recapture, illumines his disinterested public service. Lasting renown does not rest on meanness or littleness, no matter how cleverly pursued. Aside from all else, Hamilton was creative in the noble sphere of polity, and the true artist must be idealist.

Much of Hamilton's doctrine found its way into the Constitution, partly because he had early and long urged the general objects, and also because of what he recommended on the floor. His pristine proposals, though known by him to be ineligible as he made them, more than tinctured the prescriptions of others and made for greater strength in the central government than would otherwise have been approved. If to some, of opposite views, he seemed arrogant in the beginning, these must have been drawn to him as he labored manfully in later sessions for the best solution obtainable. This cordial spirit, in no wise egotistical, led him to declare at the end that no man's views were farther from the finished Constitution than his were known to be, but that for the sake of unity and practicality he endorsed it gladly and begged abstaining colleagues to join him. Though self-confident to a remarkable degree, he accepted compromises at many critical points in his public career, and it is for these concessions that he is honored almost as much as for his original contentions.

He next demonstrated to the whole country, had it but known, with what gratitude he could take the half loaf rather than go without bread. Earlier, he had forecast that any improved plan of a constitution ought to be explained and defended by sensible writings in order to secure for it necessary popular support. The Constitution had been arrived at behind closed doors, a procedure which Hamilton approved as the only feasible mode, for the utterances of members, and the changes of utterance, would have been misunderstood, with harmful results, if reported to the country while debates were in progress. Indeed, deliberations might have been widely discredited from the start, for almost of one accord delegates had disregarded their instructions to amend the Articles of Confederation, and had projected a far more consolidated government. Now a finished document was unveiled for ratification by states which found their favorite political pretensions canceled. Accept this, and no longer could states dishonor requests of Congress for revenue, jockey commerce for local benefit, issue paper money, or by less indirect means violate the obligations of debt. Participants in framing the Constitution later referred to it as amounting to a second revolution in the history of the country.

Watching the choice of opponents to sit in the New York convention, Hamilton had abundant reason to prepare for a critical contest over the Constitution in his own state. If the forces of Governor Clinton were to be prevented from swift and sure rejection, the proposed fundamental law must be publicly analyzed to dissipate fears and banish bias with reason. Forthwith Hamilton, Madison (who was in New York attending Congress), and Jay commenced in the newspapers the series of persuasive essays signed with the one signature "Publius." As they began to take effect, the purpose was broadened to win to the Constitution the people of other states as well. Hamilton wrote two thirds of the total number. Probably no such exposition, in American history, ever helped fix so decisive a result. Dashed off in rapid succession, inspired by imminent demand, these "Federalist" papers, as they came to be called, have since been taken as an authoritative interpretation of our scheme of government.

They were far removed from modern methods of mass appeal. They did not rely upon prestige of a personage, for they long remained anonymous. They coined no slogans, diverted passions to no whipping-boy. No disarming entertainment to tune the ear for a singing commercial. In these degenerate days we may pause to ask how so literate a performance as *The Federalist* could provoke so solid a response. In the absence of radio, television, picture tabloids, and fetching propaganda techniques, the habit of reading, reflection, and man-to-man discussion was cultivated. By these essays the features of the Constitution were made familiar and grateful, much as, by contrast, not long ago the face of a United States senator in inquisitorial action was rendered distasteful to millions with surprising consequence.

The earnestness and wisdom with which Hamilton and his colleagues argued in *The Federalist* carried conviction. One of the softer impeachments of Hamilton is that, egotistical and imperious, he lacked popular appeal, the common touch. Superficially, maybe so. But it is to be remembered that he was chief author of this most successful effort to win friends and influence people. Moreover, as in his vote for the Constitution in the Philadelphia convention, preparation of *The Federalist* was with him an act of compromise, an abrogation of anything like stubborn dogma. The whole procedure of approval of the Constitution, in which he figured so dramatically, was democratic so far as the election laws of the time permitted. In the end the states, in their individual capacities, could take it or leave it, and three of the most important—Massachusetts, Virginia, and New York—almost left it. In this crisis a superb mind, warm heart, and aroused purpose served the turn. Severe critics have charged that all was calculated to enthrone property and privilege under false pretenses. The last humiliation to which too-clever historians will ever be brought is the admission of simple sincerity. Hamilton's actions, when swayed by party as distinct from the public good—and there were such occasions—failed, or, worse than that, invited the opposite result. By contrast, when he ran counter to popular clamor for what he believed to be the general good, he was apt to achieve his aim. His life celebrated the success of moral force, and it is a disservice to truth to tell his story otherwise.

All that we have rehearsed leads up to the finest victory of Hamilton's early manhood. This was in winning New York to the new nation. He proved to be the prophet with honor in his own country. It is proper to compare the ratifying convention at Pough-keepsie with that meeting simultaneously at Richmond and the earlier one at Boston. All three were stressful, but at Poughkeepsie the odds against the Constitution were heaviest. In Massachusetts Sam Adams was the most celebrated of the oracles who did not find favorable signs in the viscera. He was justly respected, but Massachusetts had recently given the most conspicuous demonstration, in Shays's rebellion, of the incapacity of a state to maintain law and keep the peace. A farmer—"plough-jogger" he called himself—from the heart of the Shays country, expressed in the Massachusetts convention the sovereign conviction that only the Constitution promised protection against the dismaying disorders that all had witnessed. Moreover, if the New Union was rejected, Massachusetts was the chief of the New England states threatened with being sucked back into British allegiance and incorporation into Canada.

In Virginia the opposition met by Madison and his friends was more powerfully led. It is enough to mention Patrick Henry who had refused to attend the Philadelphia convention and George Mason who liked so little what he heard there that he refused to sign the Constitution. But the declamation of Henry and the reservations of Mason were more than offset not only by the indefatigable efforts of Madison, Marshall, and others. Governor Randolph had repented of his recalcitrancy, and pled for approval. Washington would surely be President, and was as palpably a member of the convention as had he sat in the midst.

In New York the antagonism was perfectly organized, more massive, and saving elements observable elsewhere were missing. In the beginning only nineteen delegates were for the Constitution, twice as many were for rejection, and these proportions held far into the debates and voting. Governor Clinton, unlike Hancock and Randolph, was the champion of the enemy, with his cohort drilled to protect state autonomy. He had not been a general in the Revolution for nothing. His chosen spokesman on the convention floor was Melancton Smith, as cool and pointed as Patrick Henry was furious and irrelevant. Smith was seconded by John Lansing, Jr., the rising lawyer who with Robert Yates had turned his back on the making of the Constitution in the first place. Clinton, in command of his overwhelming majority, had no doubt of defeating the Constitution outright by an early vote on the whole, by calling for a new convention of the states, or, at worst, by making adherence conditional on alterations in the instrument that would continue the old pernicious anemia.

And yet to have New York join was essential to the operation of the new nation. Otherwise the country would have been cut in two. Remember that the extreme northern and southern portions along the Atlantic strip counted for little. Georgia was only potentially populous and powerful. New Hampshire was a few settlements. Vermont did not exist except in the demands of Green Mountain Boys who were fending off the claims of New Hampshire and New York, at the same time carrying on sporadic but ominous conversation with Canada. Doubts of North Carolina proved well founded. If Virginia did not ratify, as seemed too likely, and New York flung out, that left only Pennsylvania as a distant stepping-stone between New England and South Carolina, for New Jersey, Delaware, and Maryland were ancillary. Therefore the battle at Poughkeepsie was more than for New York. It was for a united America.

Governor Clinton was too confident, and as the convention opened let the pro-Constitution fighters get in under his guard. This was by agreeing to the first resolution offered, which was that the document should be debated clause by clause before a vote was taken on the entire instrument. This gave the chance for reason, persuasion, and for delay while Virginia might come in and act as a pry on New York. The manuscript of the brief resolution is preserved with other convention papers in the New-York Historical Society. Significantly, it is in the two hands of Hamilton and his principal colleague, Robert R. Livingston. We can see them putting their heads together for a momentous object. Hamilton had the loyal help of others, including John Jay and James Duane, but throughout he generaled the struggle. He smote in center, darted to the flanks, brought up all reserves he could muster. In his whole life his resources of brain and nerve and feeling were never so completely in play. In contrast to his self-conscious deliverance at Philadelphia, Hamilton forgot himself in his single determination that the convention at Poughkeepsie should never rise until New York was unequivocally in the union.

Hamilton was fully prepared. Eight years earlier, before York-town insured military victory, he had concerted with this same Duane for a new national government that would promise political triumph. Three years along, he and Schuyler had induced New York to prod Congress for a constitutional renovation. At Annapolis he had penned the call for the Philadelphia convention. Here he had learned more than he taught. His greatest lesson was subordination of himself to a practicable plan to save America. His *Federalist* arguments gave him his own treatise ready to hand. He knew it all by heart, but every utterance at Poughkeepsie was informed with original vigor, was bent to the strategic demands of the moment. He used no tricks, spared no opponent, and was himself not spared, for his extremest sallies at Philadelphia were flung in his face by enemies with good memories.

He had arranged with Sullivan for an express from Portsmouth to announce New Hampshire's adherence. This made the ninth state, and guaranteed the Constitution at least technically. This news took only potential effect in the New York convention, where the ranks of Clinton remained unbroken. Sped by arrangement between Hamilton and Madison, another rider brought the anxiously awaited word that Virginia had come in. As Hamilton proclaimed the dispatch Clinton, in the midst of a speech, lost his hearers.

Perhaps ratification by Virginia, as we look back, turned the tide in New York. At the time chief opponents said not, and for days afterward Hamilton and his friends must hammer away. They rejected any conditional approval, beat off every specious overture. At long last their courage was rewarded when Melancton Smith, with candor that did him honor, acknowledged himself convinced for the Constitution. Lesser men, notably Gilbert Livingston, played their part in breaking away from Clinton, who stood adamant to the end when the huge majority against was turned to the precious majority of three in favor of ratification. Hamilton could afford to agree in recommendations by New York for early amendment. The victory had been won.

New York city, in an elaborate procession of floats led by the federal ship named for Hamilton, had already celebrated the fact of union. When the young champion reached home, fatigued but flushed, the universal gratitude to him was repeated in a new demonstration. The hour was his. That was incidental. It was the practical triumph of the Revolution. It was the birth of the nation as the Declaration of Independence had signaled its conception.

Now remained new tasks in plenty, in which Hamilton would never relax. A fine resolve had been taken. But the piece of paper now endorsed must become a living government, equipped with means to the end. The infant must be nourished, protected, raised to self-command and to stature in the family of mankind. This would produce parental disputes that became determined party differences. Would the lusty youngster, inheritor of a continent, thrive best on liberty to find his own directions, or would he profit by deliberate molding lest inexperience undo his promise?

These two philosophies, equally solicitous, have persisted in our national history. By quirk of fate the political parties espousing them have changed places. The followers of Jefferson, inspired by the liberty of Locke and finding fresh confirmation in early manifestations of the French Revolution, are persuaded that the rights of man are promoted by more instead of less government. On the other hand, devotees of Hamilton, who shared the apprehensions of Hobbes, who lingered in the purlieus of mercantilists, who conceived that wisdom lay in organized control, now plump for individual free will. This, of course, with shadings forced by events and the circumstances of gradual mutation.

The swap of allegiances serves to emphasize the commonplace that the two parties increasingly partake of each other, have grown to be more similar. This commenced early, for doctrine proved less influential than did economic and social development. And it is here that Hamilton's forecast and the result that he worked to bring about is conspicuous. With the exception of a dwindling minority which harbors partial or occasional cause for dissent, the country acknowledges the dominance of the national government, and, correspondingly, contraction of the sphere of the states. This is the fulfillment from Hamilton and his Federalist friends. As population has burgeoned even in proportion to area, as distances have shrunk, as mass production has superseded craftsmanship, the country has become knit and our culture becomes more nearly homogeneous. States' rights, the fences that were erected around local differences, have become increasingly anachronistic.

Hamilton would have brought the states, doubtless too early, to the national heel, making them mere administrative units under an expanding central sovereignty. Indeed, later in life he considered that the larger states should be broken into pieces, further to insure against possible competition with national authority. But the pertinence of Hamilton's project to diminish disparate loyalties in the country is evident all around us. State governors, formerly lesser presidents in their own domains, now with one voice sue for federal subsidies. States of their own accord join in regional improvements which overlie mere political boundaries. The flow of a river determines the actions of states sharing its valley. In the Great Depression of the 'thirties states became insolvent, could not put bread and cheese in the mouths of their people. Their vaunted sovereignties then suffered a blow from which they can never recover.

Hamilton hoped to have the national government the magnet, the interests and therefore inclination of all the people assimilated to its strength. When, in the midst of economic collapse, only national power could extend relief, old inhibitions founded on traditions of localism disappeared. Hamilton's prophecies were coming to pass, his purposes were being justified. The way was opened to a new scale of action for Congress, so different in degree as to be different in kind. If the national legislature could rescue not only millions of the unemployed and the aged, but set up a breadline for business and for the farmers, could it not, must it not, undertake preventive measures as well? The national government became, as Hamilton had wished and foreseen, the planning agency, promoting this sector of the economy, restraining that, coordinating all. The "welfare state" has been used as a term of reproach, approximating to the "slave state." However employed, the phrase contemplates national supremacy. Government responsibility and enterprise is shorn of the imputed evil connotation if we think of it as the democratic organization of our capacities for the common, which includes the individual, benefit.

This is not to say that local and regional divergencies of habit and interest and preference do not exist, or that they should not be consulted, or should not be protected against blanket legislation issuing from Washington. Or that the federal judiciary, so much a dependence of Hamilton's system, should be able to nullify state legislation arbitrarily. This has not happened and is most unlikely ever to happen. As Hamilton remonstrated more than once, we must not, in the heat of argument, "terrify with imaginary dangers." What has gone forward over many years with approval of the American people is the establishment of certain minima judged necessary to the health, prosperity, and safety of the nation. When states, by their incapacity or intransigence, imperil the welfare of the country, they must be aided or commanded to conform to national standards.

The issue at the Poughkeepsie convention was that of state against nation. Governor George Clinton was so proud of his bailiwick that we feel an element of compassion in his defeat. But in antagonizing the Constitution and national unity he would sacrifice the greater to the lesser claim. Though he was overcome by Hamilton, and the union was made a fact, others, with more pretension to philosophy, sought to qualify national obligation. Kentucky and Virginia resolutions, mutterings at Hartford and nullification in South Carolina, led on to secession and civil war. In our own day we must be treated to rehearsal of this regretful history in the imprecations and threats of southern states against national authority. That trading ship that tied up to the Jamestown trees and supplied the colonists with slaves brought us a cargo of national sorrow. Not the Negroes, but their status formed the calamity. Madison knew, even better than Hamilton, that slavery would prove superior to all else in producing dissension in the nation. Is it too harsh to say that afterward, in changing from nationalist to sectionalist, Madison himself fell victim to the evil?

We have come a long way in remedy of wrongs to Negroes, wrongs to whites. Are we to witness now attempted revival of "interposition" by the white South, the state to stand against the patient verdict of the nation? Though he has been dead a century and a half, Alexander Hamilton made this impossible. His dust is valiant. As a southerner born and bred, with not a Yankee in my acknowledged ancestry on either side, I would say to my defiant brethren below the Potomac: Do not feel that you are made to suffer under compulsion. Hamilton's passion was the expanding prosperity of happiness of the American people. Before we recoil too far at reproof, maybe we can remember to share in his noble hope.

Finance Minister

To the President, Directors & Company of the Bank of New York.

Pay to Samuel Meredith Treasurer of
the United States, or Order, the Sum of
Twenty thousand Dollars being the A-
mount of a Loan agreed to be made by the said
Bank to the Secretary at War, in pursuance of
an Appropriation made by an Act of Congress
of the twentieth day of August 1789: for
which this shall be your Warrant.

Given under my Hand and
the Seal of the Treasury on the
thirteenth day of September 1789

Alexander Hamilton
Secretary of the Treasury.

Countersigned by

Nch Eveleigh Compt.

No. 1.

Dollars 20,000.

Entered in the Register
Office this 13 day of
September 1789.
Joseph Nourse Regr

U.S. Warrant No. 1, the first drawn by the national Treasury. Reproduced by courtesy of the Bank of New York, which Hamilton helped to establish and which aided him in early administration of the finances.

$\mathcal{H}$AMILTON's reports on public credit, mint, bank, and manufactures proposed "means to prosperity." All were founded on the idea that national wealth resides in effective social organization. He was induced to this by the preceding political confusion and economic depression which stood in contrast to the potential capacities of a sparse population in a young country of rich latent resources. He was influenced, too, by the precepts of mercantilism. These continued to be received in advanced countries, including France and Britain where protest against governmental intervention were yet in the mouths of philosophers rather than in the acts of statesmen. Hamilton was impressed by the uses of coordination of effort, which must be deliberate, planned, and in a degree coercive. At that beginning stage in American development he was unwilling to trust to individual motive and preference, as expressed, in the economic sphere, in laissez faire, or, politically, in the rights of man. Freedom of private choice was too apt to result in disruption; the "unseen hand" that would turn selfish advantage into public benefit was too problematical in its operation.

Thus Hamilton was a collectivist in the best mercantilist tradition of utilizing governmental guidance, with restraint here and promotion there, rather than in the sense of socialists, who came later with a theory of history and a strong ethical insistence. His system was grounded in technical considerations, not in those of class antagonism. Combination of all elements of the community for national development was his aim. A varied economy, through public inducement, would favor mutual gains of farmers, merchants, manufacturers, and financiers. Economic self-reliance, even self-sufficiency, would insure against military threat. His scheme amounted to what we now call a "mixed economy," combining governmental with individual initiative. He by no means underestimated the fecundity of the latter, but private enterprise was to be invited and protected by agency of society. At the same time, competent groups in the community, knowing on which side their bread was buttered, would support government.

Shortly after his day the Western world abandoned the preference for social control to which he held, though the departure was louder in profession than in practice. Adam Smith, James Watt, and Thomas Jefferson were the heralds and heroes of the system of free-will in economy and polity. However, in addition to numerous regulative institutions which survived—notably trade tariffs—these same countries, with one accord, less than a century and a half later reembraced the system of cooperation, and with planning much more explicit and pervasive than previously. Much of Hamilton's thought is celebrated in this return to reliance on governmental authority for prosperity and safety.

Of course the New Deal of the nineteen-thirties was the conspicuous illustration in the United States. It was as though an unseen Brain Truster counseled Franklin Roosevelt; a ghostly chair was drawn to his cabinet table. Only positive government could rescue from dismaying depression. Vigor in the executive must be matched by latitude in the legislature. The states were incapable of coping with the national, indeed international, economic collapse. The Constitution must be broadly interpreted to enable the central power to serve the general welfare. Constricted credit must be relaxed, circulation must be multiplied and quickened. The federal government must become the partner of farmers, merchants, manufacturers, and bankers. Public debt would not be dangerous if it was the means of arousing the national energies. Besetting fear must be dispelled by confidence in America's future. To this psychological lift, resourceful planning must be added. Economic behavior must conform to exigency, not to supposed immutable laws.

A Democratic administration was inspired by the maxims of Thomas Jefferson and of Woodrow Wilson, but also was reverting to the preachments of the chief of the Federalists. By the same sign the Republican party, running back historically through Whigs to Federalists, had been retired from responsibility because it had fallen on inhibitions which could not meet the emergency. To be sure, in the long interval the problem had increased in magnitude and new elements entered into the solution. Particularly, direct relief must be offered to the millions of unemployed. But an accurate New Deal primer could be taken from Hamilton's advocacies. That his spirit was reanimated in Franklin Roosevelt's first term of office seems manifest. This was not an accidental twist of fate. Hamilton foresaw that with growth of population, improved means of communication, and expansion of machine industry localities and states would become interdependent. Their peculiarities would diminish or disappear. The country would be integrated, to a degree standardized in its parts. Men would look to the national government as the competent authority.

It is enough to remind of the burgeoning of the federal function in banking, control of commerce, and public works. States, once so mindful of their autonomy, would blur their frontiers in regional undertakings such as the Tennessee Valley Authority. We used to learn in school to bound the states, and to repeat the names of the state capitals. That quaint geography is forgotten. All of the governors must meet together to draw the country's notice, and what they discuss is, in one form or another, national subventions to their commonwealths. One who lived in Maryland during the Great Depression learned the irony of the prideful slogan of "Maryland Free State." The long-time governor had been considered a hopeful contender for the presidential nomination because he championed states' rights. Disillusion followed economic debacle. Maryland's chief freedom was that her capital lay closest to the office of Harry Hopkins in Washington.

Having remarked how much the New Deal had in common with Hamilton, the similarities between Lord Keynes and Hamilton may be taken for granted, since Keynes was the doctrinal patron of the New Deal. However, the correspondence of these two, each the foremost economic statesman of his country and time, serves fur-

ther to show Hamilton's prescience. Both treated economics as a
skill, not a science; as changing policy, not permanent principle.
Hamilton, with far less theoretical equipment, and not burdened
with tradition, swiftly dismissed what he found inapplicable to his
situation. Keynes was laborious in modifications, but he too was
denying dicta that hampered his purpose. Each put requirements of
his own nation first. Though Keynes, in his later phase, notably of
the Bretton Woods conference, went further to devise an international comity, the inescapable demands of autonomy of associated
countries were conciliated. Both knew that wealth, or prosperity,
and economic progress spring from social organization. In this respect Keynes had an advantage over Hamilton for he represented
a people politically practiced, whereas Hamilton contended with
political inexperience. On the other hand Hamilton's task was sim-
pler. He planned for accumulation of capital, while Keynes was
plagued with over-accumulation. Too little is more readily dealt
with than too much. One recalls the quandary of a simple-minded
sailor; if his rope was too short he could splice it, but what did he
do if it was overlong?

Hamilton's fiscal planning, at once bold and judicious, is the more
remarkable when we remember the difficulties under which he
worked. The department of the Treasury must be organized, officers chosen, an accounting system established. This would have
presented problems in any case, but all must be accomplished amidst
the detritus of the Board of Treasury of the Confederation. William Duer, the first Assistant Secretary, was a holdover from the
previous period of accumulated confusion. Though his reputation
at the time was high, he proved a poor choice. With his enterprising temper, he may have contributed to the sweep of Hamilton's
proposals, and his knowledge of previous mistakes may have been
serviceable. But his bad judgment included misconduct in office
which, if generally known at the time, would have compromised
the integrity of the Treasury in its critical beginnings. Fortunately,
his tenure was brief, though his departure in itself was an interrup-

tion. Everleigh, the comptroller, was ill and absent much before his death, which threw additional burdens on Wolcott, the auditor, until the latter succeeded to the post. Hamilton's dislike of Tench Coxe, for his personal and political disloyalty, became an impediment in Treasury operation.

Removal of records and personnel of the department to the new seat of government at Philadelphia was troublesome. While preparing his principal reports Hamilton was excessively engaged in guiding promotion of the Society for Useful Manufactures at the falls of the Passaic (Paterson, New Jersey). This over-ambitious project suffered from inexperience, the mismanagement of Duer, and the visionary engineering schemes of L'Enfant. Hamilton was at fault in the selection of these friends. He was obliged repeatedly to step in, usually to mitigate the results of costly errors in the affairs of this first pretentious industrial corporation. This was the period of his infighting with Jefferson, disruptive in the cabinet and unseemly in the press. Further, he must defend his conduct of the Treasury against a noisy attack in Congress. Another distraction had no excuse except the frailty of the human frame. This was his liaison, in 1791–92, with a Mrs. Reynolds, which led to blackmailing of Hamilton by her husband, and to potential political complications. How he combined the tearful entreaties of Maria, the expensive exactions of her spouse, the suspicions of congressmen who became privy to his lapse, and, at the same time, the purposeful conduct of the Treasury passes understanding. He had abundant reason to repent his brief infatuation—in disgust, depletion of pocket, fear of exposure, and tax on his attention.

To cap all, the Philadelphia yellow-fever epidemic of 1793 disorganized the Treasury force, as is painfully clear in Wolcott's manly efforts to prevent complete stoppage of business. Hamilton fell ill of the disease, was rescued by the ministrations of his old friend Dr. Edward Stevens, but was compelled to leave the scene to recuperate. The following year a large block of the Secretary's time went to quelling the Whisky Insurrection, for he accompanied the troops to Pittsburgh. The refusal of western Pennsylvania distillers to pay the excise raised a problem less fiscal than political and military, so it will be treated later.

Hamilton always prized the part that excellent administration could play in making legislation acceptable. His stress on efficient public housekeeping was novel in his day, for men preferred to argue about political rights and oppressions, and did not descend to consider convenient compliance with law. Hamilton's perception that many solutions lay in just procedures of enforcement anticipated a vast development in our polity. The enlarged role of the executive, as compared with the legislative and judicial functions, has produced a whole new area, administrative law, unsuspected by our forefathers. Friedrich List, more than a century ago, with his special experience in Europe and impressed by Hamilton's example, was fully aware of expansion of the police power. Marx, of course, carried farther the idea of public management.

We are assured that Hamilton's internal organization of the Treasury is what exists today, enormously elaborated. He arranged, and was at pains to explain, checks of one officer on another to secure at once dispatch of business and accountability. When the Treasury had as yet next to no income, confidence and purpose were required to lay an enduring foundation of departmental controls. Of course the grand confusion that he inherited was sufficient prompting to reform. From the first Hamilton proved himself an excellent administrator. A decade before, he had urged the importance of resting responsibility for chief departments on competent individual heads. In the event he made himself fully answerable to his plan. Inevitably, in conducting the office which had the largest staff and the greatest amount of business, slips happened. Though critics in Congress had hawk eyes for any inadvertence, much less dereliction in the Treasury, the instances were so few that we may readily count them. Once the Senate complained that Hamilton did not produce a petition supposed to have been lodged in the Treasury. He explained that if ever there it could not be found, and gave the mitigating circumstances. Again, a dismissed clerk bore tales which melted on scrutiny. Charges in the House that the Secretary had exceeded his discretionary authority had more to do with politics than with the policing of his office. In every case he answered fully; his spirited animadversions were called by some gratuitous, but they showed his instant solicitude for his reputation.

Hamilton was impatient of legislative disputes, knowing that the test of utility would come in practical application of measures. Firmness, combined with flexibility, would reconcile theoretical differences, and remove them as obstacles. This inevitably formed a component of his program of positive government. He was mindful of the evils of bureaucracy, and flinched even more from centralized dictation which we call fascism. He was quick to exercise authority properly bestowed, but was equally determined to stop short of its abuse.

When we extol the wisdom of Hamilton's proposals for revenue, debt service, currency, and industrial promotion we recognize only part of his labors in the Treasury. He zealously devised regulations covering all contacts of his department with the people. The large number of Treasury circulars, often originally drawn and afterward modified by him, and his meticulous correspondence concerning everyday problems in great variety form a little known but revealing archive. Relating as they do to the points of impact of the new central government upon the citizen, they could induce passivity or provoke discord. It was too much to hope that the deftest extraction from a person's pocket would be popular. It is only decent, we know, to object to taxes. But he studied the art of "plucking the goose with minimum squawk." He always cited the law, but consulted the spirit as well as the letter in his use of administrative discretion. The pains to which he went to suit reason to requirement must be studied in their array to be appreciated. The modifications in levy and collection of the excise to meet the convenience of western distillers is only the most conspicuous instance; the customs gave rise to more if less portentous problems. Additional bills, as they were presented to Congress, were bound to reflect, in their reception, the good or bad reaction of the people to laws already in operation. One opines that were Hamilton in the Treasury now the income tax forms would bear his scrutiny and revision. Of course all of these operations are enormously more complicated and massive than in the beginning, but also he had to contend with novelty that readily called out repugnance. A sovereign rule with him was to aim for simplicity and certainty. He stopped short of impracticable precision, resolving the last vexations arbitrarily in favor of the citizen.

The administrative rubs would have been more except for the prosperity of the country which greeted entrance of the new government. This revival from depression of the middle 'eighties was providential. It was partly owing to the Constitution and confidence in Washington's presidency, which hastened a natural recuperation. Eager demand for farm staples at good prices, ampler credit, active commerce soon reaching to the first adventures upon China lubricated the political machine. The financial panic of 1791–92, centering in New York city, was brief, and was rightly set down to overcommitment in speculation.

We have spoken of handicaps of Hamilton in organizing and conducting the Treasury. He also had helps within his department. John Adams, in his later dislike of Hamilton, said that the work of the Treasury was done by associates, for which the Secretary took credit while he indulged himself in pleasures of society. Nothing could be farther from the truth. For what had he prepared through previous years if not to give government reality, or, as he said, not only a soul, but instruments for acting? The formation and operation of the Treasury bears his impress in scope and in detail. It was the mark of good management, not of bad, that he used the talents of his subordinates.

Walcott was his chief dependence. He had served his apprenticeship at the Pay-Table of Connecticut, ending as comptroller of his native state. Hamilton himself, in recommending Wolcott to President Washington for advancement, in April, 1791, was the first to declare his competent knowledge of business and faculty for order and arrangement: "Indeed I ought to say, that I owe very much of whatever success may have attended the merely executive operations of the department to Mr. Wolcott. . . ." Wolcott's Treasury papers, as for example his response to Hamilton's request for a plan for keeping the accounts of the funded debt, in March, 1790, abundantly illustrate this. Requisitions upon the industry and talents of Tench Coxe are plainest in the Report on Manufactures, and when a large cache of Coxe's manuscripts, now privately held, shall become available for examination, his contribution to this and other documents will doubtless be further demonstrated. After routine regulations had been given their first form, and adjusted to experience, clerks of course carried on. Hamilton's excellence as an administrator is illustrated throughout. But beyond that he drew breath for the Treasury, and not only while he was in it, but to a lesser degree afterward as Wolcott, his successor, referred puzzles to his solution.

Hamilton was criticized for gratuitous assumption of responsibility in other chief departments of the new federal administration, notably interference in foreign affairs. He was fertile in ideas, by his nature took initiative, valued the interconnection of all policies. Also, most of the business of the national executive, and of the legislature, clustered in the Treasury bailiwick. Hamilton was in fact, if not in name, the chief of the cabinet ministers. After he resigned as Secretary of the Treasury he continued, for the remainder of President Washington's second term, almost as an unofficial member of the cabinet. For several reasons, mainly Washington's reliance on him, this did no harm, but good, supplying continuity in policies which Hamilton had fashioned. However, his behind-the-scenes manipulation of Adams' cabinet was ill-considered, and led to grief for all concerned. Mitigations may be offered. Heads of departments were not then expected automatically to resign when a new president came in. Adams was prone to absent himself from capital and cabinet when Congress was not in session, tempting his subordinates to seek other counsel. But Hamilton overstepped the line of propriety, indeed of candor.

Hamilton's work, indeed that of the Federalists while they remained in power, was preparatory. He spied out the land in which
others, after him, would dwell. In the Treasury his task was institutional, not philosophical. He was like Martha in the New Testa-
ment, concerned about many things. He freed his successors to
choose, like Mary, the better part, which was the realization of
America's political promise. His service was in devising ways and
means. In modern phrase, he retooled the country for enhanced
production. He constructed implements rather than ideals. Compare his first Report on the Public Credit with the Declaration of
Independence or with Lincoln's second inaugural. In all three cases
the exigency was pressing. But the solution for which Hamilton
was called upon taxed contrivance more than courage to announce
a new epoch in history, as with Jefferson, or compassion and renewed national resolve, as with Lincoln. Hamilton's prescription
for besetting ills, as measured against the others, was mundane, not
of the spirit; was worldly, not eternal.

The contrast—and other monuments among American state
papers might be selected—is only roughly accurate. But it serves
to illustrate a fact which we meet in estimating Hamilton's place in
American history. He stands, in reputation, among the giants, but
his head is not in the clouds. Posterity has assigned him a position
of importance, but lacking the éclat of some of his fellows. The
recognition accorded him has a certain plus, a credit bonus tossed
in because his fiscal achievements, more readily honored than understood, are held to contain an element of the miraculous, the
touch of genius, evidence of the divine spark. This is as much a
willing confession of incapacity on the part of the beholder as of
praise for the object admired. Hamilton is regarded as a provider,
not a prophet.

If this be a fair statement of educated opinion, is it just? Probably
so, because Hamilton's concern was national, not universal, was
specific more than general. Patriotism, however ardent, is less than
aspiration for the happiness of mankind. Why, then, do we accord
to Washington his peculiar primacy? Aside from externals, the

grandeur of Washington is in moral commitment that transcended particular goals. His pledge was sacrificial. This much said, extenuations respecting Hamilton crowd for recognition. They center in the role he chose to occupy, that of making independence viable. Without his contributions to policy, political and economic, the sublimest hopes of others might have vaporized. In the postwar pause, and reaching into the next decades, someone must fashion machinery for rescue and progress. Someone must be engineer of the new structure, and not only plan but execute it. He must be nurse to the infant republic, nourishing it to establishment in ways at once imaginative and practical. Nor could this effort be successful unless informed with liberal views. Hamilton fixed his purpose upon creating a vigorous, enduring nation. This was his lodestar in all his strivings. His ingenuity, manifest in devices for every department of the public life, sprang from this central obsession. It was his will which found the way.

All of Hamilton's work belonged to some special occasion, was in response to a particular need of the time. He did not construct a comprehensive system, and we need not lament that his intention of some day preparing a treatise on government (presumably abstract as compared with *The Federalist*), was not realized. This does not mean that his reasoning was opportunist, that his arguments were mere tracts. His several objects were connected, each aided the next. He buttressed his advocacies with appeal to the past and future as well as to the present. Everything was to be done, so that philosophical speculation, had he been so inclined, must wait upon the task in hand.

Nor were contemporary critics in any doubt about his animating desire. No matter how detailed the objectives urged against his proposals for funding legislation, approval of a foreign treaty, or scope of the federal courts, one cannot miss, in the complicated debates, the true intention of his opponents. They were not innocents, did not permit themselves to be beguiled by particulars, or confuse themselves on false scents. They paid the author the compliment of perceiving that the bits and pieces formed a mosaic. Their thrusts

at his principles rather than his program were clever in more ways
than one. On particulars of taxes, trade, currency, and their proper
administration, his enemies had small chance of matching his knowledge and wisdom. They could not score with important revisions.
It is obvious, in the backward look, that legislative objection to this
or that feature of one of Hamilton's Treasury reports and bills
amounted generally to mere cavil. For he had anticipated exceptions that might be taken to his provisions and argued them away.
He had thought out his schemes in the first instance. They were
articulated, internally and with respect to each other. Deletions
could be made, but not many substantive amendments.

The predigested quality added to the fact that protracted, lively
discussion of an interest rate of 6 percent against Hamilton's 4
percent, or a shorter span for the Bank of the United States, was
shadow-boxing. The acknowledged issue always was, do we want
to build a competent federal government, or do we intend to
salvage authority for the individual states? By the same token, as-
sailants of the Secretary's measures are to be judged by their political premises, not by their offerings on fiscal or monetary strategy.
Thus viewed, in the light of subsequent history they were mistaken.
The temptation to the position they adopted was evident. Natural
law was a political tenet before laissez faire became an economic
maxim. Many devoted men are equal to one fine effort, but are
unable to address themselves to a further accomplishment made
necessary by the first. Separation from England exhausted their
resolution, so that insuring solvency and safety for the new nation
found them without resources. Attachment to states' rights was
rendered plausible by geography, for distance begot peculiarity of
culture. Preference for being a big fish in a little pond is no novelty.
Local pride is a positive virtue, and insistence on a genuine degree
of local autonomy has better philosophical pretensions.

However, when all allowances are made, the anti-Federalists, at
that beginning stage of our national development, were lacking
in insight. One feels little compunction in applying this dictum to
the boisterous Jackson of Georgia, Findley of the over-mountain

reaches of Pennsylvania, or to Giles of Virginia who at this time was frankly obstructionist. But it seems a hard saying as descriptive of Madison, Jefferson, and some others of less capacity, say Monroe and George Clinton. One reflects that several of those named, later on, confronted by major responsibility and taught by experience, turned much more national in word and deed. Nevertheless, at the time with which we are dealing, they made the wrong guess, or set up an erroneous order of priorities. Had they succeeded, they would have penalized central authority more than they protected states' rights. Hamilton said over and over again, not bitterly but simply declaring a fact, that attachment to the states, for the foreseeable future, threatened to deny necessary powers to Congress. With a large area, sparse population, and an experimental Constitution, the anti-Federalists might have rested assured that possession was nine points of the law, that inertia worked in their behalf.

One who seeks to define Hamilton's place has his own battles without entering the contest between biographers of Jefferson and of Madison as to which of these was teacher and which was taught. Though there are pointers to the contrary, as it was Madison, rather than Jefferson, who reversed himself in the early 'nineties, it is plausible to suppose that his fellow Virginian was his magnet. Whether Madison chose to battle in the open, or was deftly nudged into the exposed quarter by his colleague, his legislative opposition to Treasury measures was to Hamilton a blessing in disguise. Hamilton's proposals were tested against the most formidable analysis they could meet from the opposition, and were approved. To know the superiority of Madison to Jefferson in this assault, compare the former's argument in the House against the bank with the latter's cabinet paper urging Washington to veto the bill. Granted that Madison, in the midst of floor debate, had better opportunity of selecting arguments, his brief, while intrinsically faulty, is not conjectural and irrelevant. When Madison, with persevering industry, had made his deposit, whatever else was brought against one of Hamilton's plans was peripheral and could be disposed of.

Thus challenged, the validity of Hamilton's recommendations

was proved, though those who differed from him were ever ready to collect for a new attack. Their obduracy takes on a certain dignity because so pertinacious. They never learned what has since been generally agreed, that they were trying to damage the work of a master craftsman. At the moment, ironically, familiarity with him disqualified his critics from appreciating his merits. His very versatility—meddling, they called it, in departments other than his own—diminished, in his enemies' eyes, his special fitness for his Treasury post. Time had not then awarded him his place among the world's finance ministers. In the years since, hardly anyone has questioned the appropriateness of Hamilton's Treasury expedients and advocacies. Critics have been driven, instead, to impugn his motives. Unhappily for truth, they have so far succeeded as to elevate his technical proficiency at the expense of his wisdom and public honesty. It is my hope that these lectures may do their bit to correct this misconstruction.

The scenes in Congress and in the society of the capital when Hamilton's Treasury proposals were the subjects of controversy were animated and anxious. Yet as we look back on the contest it could not be, on the part of the anti's, more than a joust. Indeed we wonder, in reviewing their assaults, whether they ever expected to fell their opponents. Hamilton and his friends were more than a match for them. First of all, an effective government was the pledge of the Constitution. The main point was conceded by the anti's when that document was ratified. The conflict was then joined on particulars. Here the Federalists, led by Hamilton, were better qualified. This is clear in the reports, the debates, newspaper comment, and the correspondence of the time. Hamilton had prepared himself for years, and in more recent intensive study, for shaping the propositions he put forward. These were in his department, the offspring of his mind and will. He had thought them through, in their scope and in detail. Those in rebuttal were on the defensive, could not do much more than plead the general issue, though they strove. They had neither the technical competence nor the moral identification of the Secretary with the expedients he urged.

It is remarkable, when one considers the hundreds of thousands of words spoken in rejoinder, that they advanced hardly an argument which had not been specifically anticipated and answered by Hamilton in submitting his recommendations. He had taken the precaution of prefacing his proposals with little essays revolving the subject in a manner that later in our national experience might have been called gratuitous. He had already shorn specific items of objectionable features, reducing them to the practicable. What remained he was ready to defend with the whole weight of precedent and resolve. His opponents had their fears, often born of sectional agrarian promptings, and they were skillful in seeking polemical advantage, but they were ill armed. The club could not parry the rapier.

Madison made himself the chief champion of the anti's. His conspicuous support of the Constitution was prepossessing in his favor, yet he exposed himself by caviling at means designed to serve agreed ends. When his superior reasoning powers were not sufficient, objections of others, though shrill, fell on inattentive ears. Nor did the newspapers, which might have raised shouts out of doors, come to the assistance of antagonists in Congress. Typically they printed Hamilton's reports *in extenso,* and, belatedly, proceedings in the House. In the newspapers I have examined, up and down the coast, more short letters from subscribers praised the Secretary than criticized him. Longer letters were few on either side, and numbers of those against the Treasury proposals betrayed evidence of issuing from the same author. On the whole, if we may judge by the newspapers, the country, even the literate portion of it, was unprepared for meaningful discussion. This is what we would expect at that juncture in the case of reports and bills which were in essential respects sophisticated and technical. The repeated complaint of enemies was that Hamilton purposely complicated his measures beyond common understanding. It is safe to say that his object was quite the other way, and that the fault lay with the disability of legislators and readers. Misunderstanding might have been avoided and the debates shortened if Hamilton had been allowed to appear before the House in presenting his reports. Some of the legislators who were afraid of his influence would have profited by his information. As it was, critics used the tactic of prejudicial political appeal, more natural than creditable.

However, Hamilton's measures were aided by satisfaction of the people in Washington's presidency and by returned prosperity. The two were popularly linked as cause and effect. From contemporary expressions outside of the House one gets the impression that Treasury recommendations were received with little intention to rebut them. Of course hostile pamphleteers, John Taylor of Caroline one of the most adept, stigmatized Hamilton's funding system and its concomitants as means whereby "the fiscal corps" profited while landholders "should groan under the burdens of government. . . ." Taylor's object was to stir political protest. He showed cardinal ignorance of the operation of Treasury institutions, the bank for instance. Approval of open discussion of public policy must tolerate disingenuous methods. But at the same time, reading Taylor and his agrarian confreres, one appreciates Hamilton's warnings against demagogues, and not all of them crude practitioners.

As we look back on those contentious times, more was accomplished than the repair of public credit. Certainly the means chosen were reasonable, almost inescapable—consolidation of debts, sinking fund for repayment, and bank to expedite Treasury and private requirements. The virtue was that a young democracy could arrive at these solutions, especially when several of them involved a liberal interpretation of a written Constitution on which the ink was scarcely dry. There has hardly been an instance in which sensible action by majority consent was so needed at the moment and so potent for the future. The episode goes a good way to reassure those who put faith in the competence of popular government.

Dean Louis M. Hacker's recent and admirable book, *Hamilton in the American Tradition*, provokes discussion of the question

how far Hamilton meant to substitute public for private motiva-
tion. Did he intend simply to prime the pump and start the flow,
after which individual capitalists and enterprisers would seize the
handle? Was he content to supply initial confidence through stability of government, the goodness of its credit, security of property, and positive encouragement by protection to manufactures
and the facility of a public bank? Did he expect to see the maxims
of Adam Smith early demonstrated in America? Was the helping
hand of government to be extended merely in an awkward interim,
until the unseen hand of private incentive would commence to
operate?

Obviously our answer must depend upon the length of time
Hamilton envisaged for governmental sponsorship and tutelage.
I am inclined to think this was long. How much free and available
capital was there in the country for investment in new, risky undertakings of size? The public demands during the Revolution had
drained it and given as receipt the mass of variegated inconvertible
paper. Before the war was over the pool was exhausted, feeding
springs had been tapped, and Congress was forced to issue new
paper to redeem old. Promise had been piled on promise. We may
easily be deceived by the eagerness and volume of speculation in
securities and wild lands about the time Hamilton took office into
thinking the readiness of liquid funds greater than was the case.
The Secretary repeatedly lamented the lack. Zestful, ingenious
acquisitiveness there was in New York, Philadelphia, Boston, and
a few other seaboard towns. But the values involved—means of
payment as well as results to be realized—were prospective. This is
evident in the correspondence and contracts of the small company
of active manipulators. With what would they buy? Why, with
depreciated securities, of which they had sufficient or could cheaply
amass more. A small first installment on shares would give an equity
which would yield handsome returns as the enterprise developed
and its stock rose in price. Most of the real money counted upon
was to come from Europe, especially Holland and France. Men of
means, as Clavière assured, "calculating the vicissitudes of Europe,"

would find it prudent to put their "dead funds" in lands in rising America. But not all investment from Europe would be in liquid form, for particularly in France many held our paper which they were glad to exchange for anything tangible or hopefully so.

Among the Americans, in favored places, was a modest mercantile capital, devoted to quick turnover by the standards of that day. A respectable group in New York had feared that the bank established there in 1784 would divert these essential funds to less proved undertakings and dissipate them, and the same apprehensions attended the proposal for the Bank of the United States. Industrial projects, if more ambitious than the shop of the local artisan, would have to attract numerous capitals, under the shelter of incorporation. The largest of these, the Society for establishing Useful Manufactures, which Hamilton in his official capacity promoted, could enlist only a few of the richest men in the largest towns. Even so, it must include a subscription by the state of New Jersey, and further depended on a lottery. Payments except of the first installment were hard to collect; physical construction, though greatly reduced from original plans, lagged, and actual production was feeble and then failed utterly. Hamilton in the event was obliged to induce bank loans by Treasury assurances to the lender, justifiable on grounds of policy rather than of principle. This was the instructive history of a project of Hamilton's own inspiration, which had the benefit of his official prestige, and at times enjoyed his active oversight. Again, as with the banks, the cry was insistent that an industrial corporation of such magnitude would injure small producers—the self-employed and their few journeymen and apprentices—forestalling their raw materials and preempting their markets.

Hamilton's Treasury proposals went far beyond fiscal tidiness. He intended by these means to insure competence and expansion of the economy. When he was making his early batch of reports, lesser industrial schemes than his own godchild died a-borning, and plants that had actually come to life failed and were closed down. These furnished sobering lessons. The financial panic of 1791–92, centering in New York city, precipitated by the ruin of Duer and deepened by the suspension of Macomb, showed how gaseous had been the bubble and how easily it was pricked. Under trying circumstances Hamilton kept his head admirably, refusing to be visibly disturbed in the early stage when signs of Treasury trembling would have quickened and spread the disaster. However, he could not but know, sorrowfully, that the investment funds displayed were mere froth.

What could be mustered for dependable progress? America was almost entirely agricultural. What men possessed was in lands, buildings, implements, and could scarcely be transmuted to liquid form. If we speak of fresh undertakings, in numbers and variety, whether for industry, transport, or new settlements, we may say there was, for investment, little in circulating media, less in instruments negotiable without sacrifice, and least in specie.

What, then, remained? Only the faith of government and the work of hands. The two were intimately connected, like Siamese twins with one blood stream; if one died the other expired. Hence Hamilton gave his whole force to rendering public debt valuable. This was the center of his system, the foundation on which he would build national progress. All else—revenue, security, banks, prices, private trade and investment—stood upon governmental credit. Thus the funding plan was his synosure. When he said that the public debt, consolidated and with provision for its redemption, could be to us a public blessing, he had in mind more than a political cement. Public pledges, inviolably fortified and perfectly negotiable, would furnish the basis of private credit, of circulating media, and be in themselves to a degree money. Safe public debt would be the wellspring of proliferating economic activity.

Consider the imagination and courage of this proposition. He turned a bane into a benefit. The millstone around our necks he made a pedestal on which to mount. Disgrace and dismay became honor and confidence. He might have yielded to the shortsighted urgings of his antagonists in Congress and an abundance of critics in the country by consenting to gross repudiation, at least of the domestic debt. Political, economic, even ethical arguments for this course were not lacking. They were specious. He was not devising a fiscal expedient. In the principles which he demanded in the Treasury he was creating a nation, and he knew it. He thought on a different plane from that of his opponents. He was more than an administrator of the finances. His proficiency as a technician in almost all respects was unquestionable. This was a source of strength both in fact and in public acceptance of his program. But beyond this he was a minister of state, combining every element in the society that would make for national advance—political union, economic energy, moral resolve. This was his glory of mind and heart.

This sounds like panegyric? I am encircling with a halo what was simply a good head? Not so. Of course his Treasury policies are reducible to specific arrangements, all familiar, in the honor and the breach, in previous fiscal history. But do not make the error of damning him with faint praise for a competent funding operation. In the bottle of funding dwelt a genie which, uncorked, would rise into a giant of national prosperity. The perception of this is what set off the master from the journeyman, the artist from the artisan. This is why his Treasury papers, especially his first report on the public credit, 1790, are national monuments. Their details—and vastly more detail appears in his correspondence in administration of his office—commend themselves to critical admiration. But in all is a presiding spirit, a power to project the national future.

I am unable to agree with the observation of William Graham Sumner that Hamilton fell victim to the fallacy of "the magic of a sinking fund" which infected the imaginations of some British writers and fiscal administrators. The passages cited do not bear out the charge. Hamilton was too penetrating to believe that debt re- tired by sinking fund purchase would go on drawing interest, and thus promote final total liquidation, in the absence of correspond- ing appropriations. He understood perfectly that there is no miracle of accumulation in a sinking fund. On the contrary, it would be enough to keep it inviolate. Repeatedly he was emphatic in warning against the temptation to raids on the sinking fund for other than its pledged object.

In all of Hamilton's Treasury proposals, political purpose was mixed with fiscal design. This was no disingenuous use of familiar means to ulterior ends. Especially at the outset of the nation, economic health was necessary to political strength, and vice versa. This blend of objects came under sharpest scrutiny in the case of the Bank of the United States. The funding system, while loudly controversial, concerned policy, not governmental principle. In that instance, options for conversion of old debt into new might be varied, interest rates could be higher or lower, state debts might be left to the separate jurisdictions or be consolidated with federal obligations. There was room for choice within a general agreement.

But the power to establish a national bank, by comparison, was fundamental to the theory of the Constitution. It posed the problem, what kind of government had been projected? Was it to be positive, with liberal interpretation of authority, or so restrictive as to deserve the name negative? This was the clash that divided patriots into parties.

While more words have been spoken and written on this than on any other constitutional theme, the cabinet opinions offered to President Washington by Jefferson and by Hamilton may stand for the remainder. The two are poles apart. Jefferson averred that "To take a single step beyond the boundaries . . . specially drawn around the powers of Congress, is to take possession of a boundless field of power, no longer susceptible of any definition. . . . Certainly no such universal power was meant to be given to them. It was intended to lace them up straightly within the enumerated powers. . . ." On the other hand, it appeared to Hamilton "that this *general principle* is *inherent* in the very definition of government, and *essential* to every step of the progress to be made by that of the United States; namely, that every power vested in a government, is, in its nature, SOVEREIGN, and includes . . . a right to employ all the means requisite, and fairly applicable, to the attainment of the *ends* of such power, and which are not precluded by restrictions and exceptions specified in the constitution, or not immoral, or not contrary to the essential ends of political society."

Whence came this contradiction of views? It did not descend from difference in learning, though Jefferson's knowledge of political philosophy, from classical times, was superior to Hamilton's. The economic historian may be allowed to fix it in the contrasting experience of these statesmen. Jefferson grew up on an agrarian frontier, in a locality yet visited by Indians—tame ones, to be sure, but with the smack of the farther wilderness about them. His school and college mates were sons of farmers. In France he enjoyed the friendship of physiocrats who found all true wealth springing from land, and who opposed to the meddling of mercantilists the free law of nature. His beloved home on a mountaintop was isolated; the fields that spread below formed a domain nearly self-sufficient. In such environment government could be minimal.

Hamilton spent all his life in seaports which lived upon traffic. The means of wealth were man-made, like shops and ships; the instruments by which these operated were social, like credit. His was an environment of people, interdependent, bound by conventional ties. Here public controls and services were essential. Jefferson's background was rural, where dwelt rights. Hamilton's was urban, lively with interests. Hamilton was a man of industrial revolution which was emerging, not of the agricultural revolution which had preceded. He was bourgeois, not a country gentleman. This mundane explanation of the divergence of leaders may be extended to embrace the sections of America which they represented, the more thickly settled and diversified North, and the sparsely populated South specialized to extracting from the soil.

Given their distinct environments, we may particularize for each man within his setting. Hamilton for more than a decade had "considered that . . . a bank is not a mere matter of private property, but a political machine of the greatest importance to the State." While yet a soldier in the Revolution he had urged on Duane and Morris a more ambitious bank than the one Morris established. The years of disrupted credit and currency had further impressed him with the need for a handmaiden of the Treasury. He rejected the Bank of North America as unequal to the function he envisioned. His report of December, 1790, proposing the Bank of the United States, opened with persuasive pages unobtrusively instructing Congress in the uses of banks in general and particularly for this country. His pains were not misplaced, as the reaction of Jefferson and others demonstrated. Jefferson, much abroad, was unfamiliar at first hand with the vexations in America with which Hamilton contended.

To Hamilton a corporation was a useful expression of governmental authority, the sponsorship of law necessary to enlist private enterprise. Hamilton was a corporate man. To Jefferson a corporation was economically repugnant and constitutionally illicit.

The principle of implied powers which Hamilton celebrated in his defense of the bank was not novel. He had not broached it in his original report, but it promptly formed the staple of debate, being championed by Ames, Sedgwick, Boudinot, and Lawrence and as flatly repudiated by their anti-Federalist opponents. The issue having been presented, Hamilton, in his argument to Washington, at once declared the effective sovereignty of the central government within its designated sphere as also of the state within its constitutional competence. The doctrine had long been a tenet with him. At this historic last moment, when the President pondered conflicting forces, Hamilton gave the rule crisp statement that carried it into our history. John Marshall, in his upholding opinion in *McCulloch vs. Maryland* a generation later, was as logical but not so spirited. Also, by 1819 Marshall was dealing with the legality of the Second Bank which had been chartered by the party which, to its sorrow, had discontinued the first. Marshall confirmed a child which Hamilton had christened. We may notice, however, that Hamilton's defense of the bank was not struck in white heat at one blow. Mrs. Hamilton long afterward related, as she surely believed, that he had written the opinion in a single night. His manuscripts show, as his letters to Washington declare, that he had been "sedululously engaged in it" for the week since he received the order to prepare it.

When a candid champion is genuinely exercised for a result, he will avoid dogmatism and concealment. He will not be afraid to put his cards on the table. This was illustrated by Hamilton in several crises of his career. In this instance, arguing for the legality of the Bank, he said quite simply: "The truth is, that difficulties on this point are inherent in the nature of the federal constitution. They result inevitably from a division of legislative power. The consequence . . . is, that there will be cases clearly within the power of the National Government, others, clearly without its power; and a third class, which will leave room for controversy and difference of opinion, and concerning which a reasonable latitude of judgment must be allowed." That was more disarming than demand.

I resist the temptation to sketch, even in barest outline, the influence of the doctrine of implied powers as the American scene has unfolded. That would take us away from Hamilton's Treasury plans as such. Everyone knows that the principle, nudged by developing needs, has received unguessed applications. As Hamilton understood, it was more than an expedient for inducing the President's signature to a particular bill. It was a theory of sovereignty within a federal constitutional system, combining freedom of government with security of law. Hamilton's doctrine of implied powers in fact reinforced Jefferson's exclamation that "the earth belongs to the living." By a liberal interpretation, the Constitution became a living, dynamic instrument. An advance claim was entered for experimentation, for new expedients to meet arising needs. A century and a quarter later, other Virginians (Glass and Wilson) sponsored a Federal Reserve banking system which was the descendant of the United States Bank that Jefferson, Madison, Giles and their friends anathematized.

A hundred and sixty-five years ago Jefferson, as one "who wished for virtuous government," complained to Washington that Hamilton was subverting the Constitution: "For, in a report on the subject of manufactures . . . it was expressly assumed that the general government has a right to exercise all the powers which may be for the *general welfare*, that is to say, all the legitimate powers of government." Since then Jefferson's political followers have familiarized us with the term "welfare state," and only those of opposite tendencies hold the name in derision. Under implied powers we extend the welfare motive to countries distant in place and politics from our own, to build up their resistance to Communism which we fear. At first blush, not much compatibility appears between the purposes of Hamilton and of Mr. Norman Thomas. And yet it was by national action, for which Hamilton and his friends cleared the way, that Mr. Thomas's socialist program has been sensibly forwarded. Indeed, the Socialist party, as such, has dwindled principally because the New Deal accepted governmental responsibility and put into effect public planning which approximated immediate socialist proposals. At present Keynes is the presiding spirit in the Western world as is Marx in much of the Eastern hemisphere. The correspondence between Keynes and Hamilton is elsewhere noted. We must mention that they shared belief in fiscal and monetary management, including emergency deficit financing, for economic stability and progress. If I suggest that there are similarities between Marx and Hamilton nobody will believe me, so I do not go into that.

Given the funded debt and Bank, furnishing facilities in credit and currency, Hamilton could expect increase in production. He pled constantly for more abundant means of exchange and quicker circulation. No aim crops up oftener in his plans. However, if advantage was to follow, government must foster variety in economic pursuits.

Hamilton's Report on Manufactures (December, 1791) best reveals him as a political economist. Though laid aside by Congress at the time, it proved the most prophetic of his proposals. Here he addressed himself, in fundamental fashion, to the means of rendering the country "opulent," that is, bringing its resources, physical and human, into fullest play. He is the national economic planner,

by far the first in our history and the most emphatic of his generation of statesmen and writers. He refuses to leave economic forces
to their natural course, but wants to "induce" variety so that agriculture, commerce, and industry may be mutually stimulating.
Throughout, his concern is for public prosperity, with private interests nourished that they may be contributory. To this end the
intervention of government is primary. He anticipated, in most
respects, developments in America a quarter-century later. His
reasoning could have served as a model for Soviet planning a
hundred and forty years afterward, as also for the Tennessee Valley Authority and current projects for modernization of many
backward countries. He rejected more of the recommendations of
Adam Smith than he adopted, and where the Scots philosopher
approximated his own thought, Hamilton went beyond him.

Hamilton refuted, for America in its then stage, the double
preference for laissez faire and sole devotion to agriculture. He dismissed the French physiocrats more summarily than Adam Smith
had done. This was by way of marking the ground for his argument. Then he was constantly concerned to convert American
partisans from the belief that we should, first and foremost, give
our energies to the extension of cultivation of the land with which
we were so abundantly endowed. He conciliated opposition—
philosophical, political, and practical—by showing how agriculture
would be best advanced by due attention to manufactures, commerce, transportation, and credit. In his effort to utilize government
to help produce rounded economic development he could not escape solicitude for farmers and planters. But he was sincerely as
well as ingeniously persuasive in their behalf. He appealed to their
interest as well as to their public wisdom.

Besides, the more dispersed the people were, the less unified
politically and the less effective the central authority would be. In
the beginning he was afraid that this country was too extensive for
republican government, though later he revised this view and approved of the Louisiana Purchase. He remained apprehensive of
local attachments, loyalty to the individual states rather than to the

nation. The more distinct the economy of the states, the more disparate must be the country's polity. The states, for him, had genuine value as proving-grounds for democratic participation by citizens, but states must not enfeeble national sway. Hamilton, with others of his persuasion, remembered vividly the distraction and cross-purposes of the period of the Confederation, which they had worked so hard to cure. While the obtrusive preference of the American people for a federal system compelled him to caution in what he said and did, his inveterate effort was to knit the country economically and politically. He looked forward to the time when pursuits and culture would be generalized and the states would be suitable administrative units with independent responsibility for not much more than internal policing. Toward the end of his life he advanced the proposal that the largest states, potentially able to threaten national authority, should be subdivided.

We may only mention his specific proposals. Manufactures should be encouraged by bounties and rewards for invention in preference to protective duties, or by a judicious combination of bounties and duties. Internal improvements to which the capacity of one or several states were unequal would claim national appropriation. The national debt might be considered "an artificial increase of capital, . . . an engine of business," and bank credit would be a further means, but foreign investment was anxiously desired. Similarly, foreign artisans would be eagerly welcomed to supplement the scarce native supply. Social costs there would be in promoting industry and sheltering American experiments against the competition of older centers, but this temporary sacrifice would be more than repaid in the expanded production, prosperity, and security of the country. The guaranteed home market for manufactures would by the same token furnish a steady demand for agricultural surpluses. Not only would division of labor in industry augment output, according to the pattern of Adam Smith, but variety of economic pursuits would open new avenues of effort and the exploitation of otherwise unguessed resources.

Was all of this argued for the benefit of manufacturing enterprisers? When their reluctance and handicaps were overcome, they would profit surely. But they were to be instruments in a plan in which government would assume the initiative. I take it that this is the correct reading of his discourse and purpose. He looked forward, ultimately, to a system of perfect liberty as the most desirable, but this would be when the economy of this country had matured, and when other nations were willing to discontinue special encouragements to their industries. Others, who came later, most notably Friedrich List, hoped for the same result after the preparatory protective stage had been accomplished.

However, the great lesson of the Report on Manufactures is over and above what has been specified. It is that the fullest economic development, especially in new countries, is the product of conscious, deliberate organization. Hamilton's followers, such as Daniel Raymond, the Careys, List, and John Rae spelled this out in what has been termed "the sociological theory of capital." Hamilton presented it in more than embryo, for, besides the particular public aids which he recommended, he pointed out that "everything tending to establish . . . permanent order in the affairs of the country" would powerfully promote "the total mass of industry." This is your true political economy.

Party Leader

pg 168.   146   New York 26 Dec. 1800

Dr —

The post of yesterday gave me the pleasure
of a letter from you. I thank you for
the communication. I trust that the letter
which I wrote you the day before the receipt
of yours will have duly reached you as
it contains some very free & confidential
observations ending in two results — 1 That
the Convention with France ought to be
ratified as the least of two evils 2 That
— on the same grounds Jefferson ought to
be preferred to Burr.

I trust the Federalists
will not finally be so mad as to vote for
the latter. I speak with an intimate &
accurate knowledge of character — His elevation
can only promote the purposes of the desperate
and profligate — My opinion may be rely'd
upon with such reserves as you shall

Y very truly
A H

[left margin:]
the world I
ought to hate
it is Jefferson —
with Burr I
have always
been personally
well. But
the public
good must I think
paramount to
very private considerations
G Morris

12812

This letter to Gouverneur Morris (December 26, 1800) is one of several in which Hamilton begged that Federalist electors give their votes to their political opponent, Jefferson, rather than bargain with Aaron Burr. Hamilton had already evidenced his profound distrust of Burr as a potential unprincipled dictator.

$\mathcal{T}$HE United States won political independence in the Revolution, but we did not secure economic self-determination until thirty years later in the War of 1812. Between these dates we were in European leading-strings. We achieved full nationality only with the fall of Napoleon. Hamilton accomplished the task of political consolidation, but our competence as a separate people waited on the economic development which Hamilton urged but had not time to effect. At the outset of our national existence the world was being made new by two dynamic forces, the industrial revolution in Britain and the political or juridical revolution in France. Together these upheavals ushered in the modern epoch. America, claiming freedom, exemplified both historic developments. In one case we were ahead of Europe, for our Declaration of Independence anticipated the Declaration of the Rights of Man. In the other case we must take lessons from abroad, patterning power machine production after the British example. However, in both respects we played a subordinate part. Distant, and our character unformed, we received rather than gave impressions. American public policy, domestic and foreign, in the period in which Hamilton was most active, was colored by events abroad, particularly by the mortal combat between Britain and France beginning in 1793. The struggle for mastery, so long as it remained ideological, may be put, too briefly, as between law and liberty, or tradition and innovation, or experience and experiment.

In America, as someone said, it was as though every man wore a sign on his forehead marking him as the partisan of one contestant or the other. Each allegiance had its strength and weakness. Those favorable to France must apologize for excesses, especially bloody in the Reign of Terror. Those drawn to England's side bore the burden of espousing our late enemy and neglecting or antagonizing our recent ally. As the conflict progressed, the reflection of hostilities in America became less acute. On the whole the Federalist position was bolstered, for it was clear that the aspiration of France for democracy had changed to a demand for dominion. Further, America loomed as the most important neutral. We had measurably established our political unity and laid the basis of our economic advance. Our agriculture staples were avidly sought by both belligerents. We stood to lose or gain by the depredations of both, directed against our commerce because aimed at each other. In parlous years of shifting fortunes in Europe, America emerged as a separate entity with distinct claims on our own account. Developing American nationality inured to the credit of the Federalist who had all along, in spite of accusation to the contrary, placed our interest foremost.

One is tempted to depict clashes in American policy in the first decade and a half of our national life in terms of differences between great protagonists, Hamilton and Jefferson. The historic opposition, otherwise nebulous and confused, becomes agreeably concrete, simple, and animated when we supply plausible dramatis personae. This mode is probably too attractive to be dislodged from popular acceptance. Yet it is vulgar in obscuring deeper motives. It is harmful in leaving the impression of a permanent antagonism of forces which were in fact complementary. Either would have been less beneficial, or positively dangerous in its tendencies, without the other. What we see arrayed are central authority and encouragement of a varied economy on the one hand, and local autonomy and principal devotion to agriculture on the other. But this was not a conflict of absolutes, for time entered as an ingredient. Broadly the Federalists, pitching their case on the need for order and control, were correct at the outset. They were pragmatic and serviceable in the first formative period. The progress of the democrats was necessarily delayed. This is symbolized in the change of their designation from anti-Federalists to Republicans. At the start they were merely negative, and fortunately so until as a people we were secure, with a roof over our heads and bread and cheese. Then they became positive when rights could be asserted without peril to primary requirements. Of course the two advocacies overlapped, and each repeatedly reappeared subsequently.

The penchant for choosing champions is further questioned if we consider certain similarities or agreements of Jefferson and Hamilton. Both praised the British constitution. Both, in the beginning, felt that we should remain neutral in the European war. Both were for the dismissal of Genêt. Jefferson entered the deal with Hamilton whereby the state debts were assumed in exchange for placement of the capital on the Potomac. Jefferson did not always belong to what Hamilton called "the disorganizing sect," for he wrote to Lafayette in the spring of 1790, "If the President can be preserved a few years till habits of authority and obedience can be established generally, we have nothing to fear." Jefferson, like Hamilton, believed in modified suffrage. On the other hand, Hamilton was adamant for unalloyed popular control of the House of Representatives. Jefferson, the declared democrat, in practice held many chattel slaves, bought and sold them. Hamilton, pictured as the apostle of privilege, was an abolitionist. Hamilton favored viable state governments, though within a sphere more restricted than Jefferson wished. It is well remembered that when Jefferson became president he used powers truly national, as in the Louisiana Purchase, which Hamilton approved, and later exercised further authority which Hamilton, had he lived, would have endorsed in principle. Other particular correspondences or approximations could be noted.

Neither must we take at face value the charges and epithets which political opponents, in the heat of controversy, flung at each other. We must not diminish the worthiness of contestants by reinvoking old quarrels. Antagonists often saw a fateful crisis where was only a passing contretemps. In this light we may take their vehemence against each other as evidence of sincerity of both.

Even in the thick of controversy, Hamilton could see that party suspicions were exaggerated. "One side appears to believe," he observed, "that there is a serious plot to overturn the State governments, and substitute a monarchy to the present republican system. The other side firmly believes that there is a serious plot to overturn the general government, and elevate the separate power of the States upon its ruins. Both sides may be equally wrong, and their mutual jealousies may be . . . causes of the appearances which mutually disturb them and sharpen them against each other." That was an accurate judgment. Later experience was to show that neither party was bent on going to extremes. Instead, they counterbalanced each other to the nation's benefit.

Hamilton and Jefferson differed materially in philosophy and policy, but "both were original, and great." The passionate attachment of each to the success of the United States is not doubted. That they viewed this object from divergent angles was our chief political blessing. Here, more than in specific provisions of the Constitution, were the true checks and balances. The Federalists, left to themselves in their zeal for harmony, would have lapsed into coercions repugnant to liberty. They gave evidence of it. The Republicans, if unopposed, would have failed to give the national government sufficient strength in the critical commencement of its career, and in enthusiasm for freedom might have invited disunion. They, too, gave more than hints of this failing. As it was, leaders of superlative capacity corrected each other, producing between them a nation combining vigor and virtue. In concluding these observations need I remind that in the end Hamilton sacrificed his party to his devotion to the country's welfare, though this meant elevating his political enemies? Familiarity with the lives of Hamilton and of Jefferson prompts the conviction that they thought better of each other than did their partisans, then or since.

The saying that politics is the art of the possible has its exceptions. The beginning of our national government is one. To many all that seemed possible was amendment of the Confederation, toning it up a little in the hope that we would muddle through to the survival of independence and union. Extent of territory, agricultural preoccupation, diversity of regions and consequent strength of local attachments all gave this counsel. Postwar depression—of land values as well as of business activity—was not only economic, but political and moral. Winning the war had seemingly unfitted us to win self-discipline. After the one critical effort we went limp. A few leaders knew that we must go on to consolidate our position, to construct a nation vigorous at home and respected abroad. In deference to the prevailing lethargy they first tried temporizing measures, such as an independent revenue for Congress and reconciliation of trade and territorial jealousies between the states.

When these partial expedients, recommended as "the possible," were disappointed, they addressed themselves to accomplishing what they familiarly referred to as a second revolution. They resolved upon the impossible. The Federalists were aided by the compactness and intelligence of their group. But they were helped by more. Reading of the times tells us that they could not have succeeded without their patriotic purpose. The supposed wisdom of historical hindsight says that property and privilege seized the desperate chance to impose a new polity. This is a half-truth, in spite of the fact that anti-Federalists stigmatized their opponents as a corrupt squadron of monocrats and "paper men," and Federalists called the others demagogues and Jacobins. Neither side was disingenuous, though as years went on party maneuver more and more obtruded.

I speak here of the Constitutional Convention, ratification by the states, and inauguration of the national government. This was a noble work of arousal, with means subordinate to ends. Nothing less than public devotion could have triumphed. Devious design would have betrayed itself. Only sincerity could succeed. Those who pressed for renovation did not consult obstacles. To be sure, in the trial they compromised, but for the sake of an over-all departure which remained intact. They did not temporize, cut and fit, adjust in the hope that some day all would come out right. Their concessions were within a framework which they held steadily before their eyes.

Perhaps the most notorious newspaper controversy in our national political history was that between Hamilton on the one hand and the close adherents of Jefferson on the other in the summer and autumn of 1792. Its asperity was sharper because of personal as well as party color. It aired the clash between the principal cabinet ministers under President Washington, who remonstrated with both to desist ere worse damage was done. The charges and countercharges swelled louder because the disputants used pseudonyms, the same writer appearing in different guises, though perceptive readers could not have been deceived as to true identities. The furious exchanges were chiefly in the *Gazette of the United States* on Hamilton's part, and in the *National Gazette* by Madison and Freneau; Jefferson preferred to have his champions take the shock of battle for him.

A couple of months earlier, when Hamilton resisted the temptation to a public fray, he declared his complaints against Jefferson and Madison in a long private letter to their Federalist fellow-Virginian, Edward Carrington. This is the most revealing short account of the divergences of parties. Suspicions of Jefferson from the start, because he accepted the Constitution only qualifiedly and was "electrified with attachment to France," soon grew into the conviction of Hamilton that Jefferson would make the government odious in order to obtain mastery of it. The defection of Madison, his former loyal collaborator in national measures, hit Hamilton harder. He refused to credit it until Madison's opposition to the funding system. But now, he declared, these foes, acting as one, meant to dislodge him, pit the states against national authority, and throw America into the embrace of France (inviting war with Britain). Men acting with Jefferson and Madison, though not these leaders themselves, designed to prostrate national and state governments alike and erect monarchy on the ruins.

Hamilton had thus far unburdened himself privately. But he soon resolved that his and the country's enemies should be exhibited to the public. He spread his accusations in the press, citing chapter and verse. Even when Washington pled for an end to the unseemly display of mutual rancors, Hamilton replied that he could not recede for the present, and in fact his pieces continued to appear for weeks afterward. The fat was in the fire. Hostile parties were to be. Fortunately conflict was increasingly transferred to elections and other fields of fairer fight than newspaper thrusts of Secretaries who sat about the same cabinet table.

It is hard to know how to distribute blame for the melee in the gazettes. Hamilton began it, if we fasten on overt action, by publishing his charge that Jefferson had bribed Freneau to fulminate against government and its honest servants. The poet-editor had been given a clerkship in Jefferson's department. Also Hamilton was friendly to Fenno, the Federalist printer, lending him money. On the other hand, apparently, Jefferson and Madison had commenced private insinuations against Hamilton. On substantive matters Hamilton had the better of the argument. His unmannerly method is mitigated by the reflection that he rightly regarded his Treasury measures as essential to the faith and progress of the national government. Nor could the states, for which his opponents spoke, prosper if the central power was faltering. Striving mightily to establish the country on a promising course, he was driven to lash out at critics who offered little construction.

As a sequel of the squabble in the press, Hamilton's critics resolved to attack from a new quarter, not newspaper columns but in Congress. They would take the initiative. They would not bandy political ideas, but would call for an investigation of Hamilton's management of the Treasury. They would be specific with their insinuating interrogatory. The result might show that he had disobeyed the legislative branch, had favored the Bank of the United States to the prejudice of French claims, had incurred unnecessary costs to the public. The President's confidence in him might be weakened, the Secretary might even be impeached. Congress would adjourn before Hamilton could submit the varied reports called for, and in the recess he would rest under injurious imputations.

The campaign of accusation was really not promising from the start. The peg on which it was hung was volunteered by Hamilton when he explained, quite as a matter of course, that he had combined certain foreign loans which Congress had supposed would be distinct in negotiation and in application. If this involved error, a guilty Secretary would not have revealed his misconduct. Jefferson inspired the assault, he and Madison drafted the resolutions, Giles introduced and defended them. But this triumvirate rushed in ignorantly. As Hamilton said in reply, if they had asked him he could have quickly set them straight on Treasury procedure and removed doubts. They preferred to advertise as a public mystery what was only their lack of penetration. They pitched the battle on Hamilton's home ground, where the familiarity was his and where he had the strongest motives for self-vindication. Could his foes have estimated the chances with detachment, they must have realized that the rebuttal would recoil upon them.

However, Hamilton had the problem of summarizing much detail in the shortest time. This was a physical feat, let alone the analysis required if the exhibits were to refute the charges implied. The accounting labor fell principally on Wolcott, who now, if never before, earned Hamilton's enduring thanks and trust. The replies which Hamilton submitted must have satisfied reasonable men not only of the honesty but of the high competence of Treasury operations. However, blindly determined to destroy Hamilton, his foes seized on technicalities in their attempt at formal censure. Even so, they sought delay to further their mischief.

The Federalists—especially William Smith, Boudinot, and Ames —were conclusive in refutation, and compelled votes before adjournment. Hamilton was handsomely upheld. The discretion he had used in departing from the letter of Congressional mandate was justified. We cannot suppose that instigators of the inquiry and attempted condemnation were ingenuous. Were they so, they failed to see that the administrator must be allowed a degree of latitude. At the beginning of our history, those jealous of national power had misgivings about the legislature, but the executive they wanted to strait-jacket. Hamilton, by his actions and advocacy, did more than anyone else to establish the executive as a coordinate function in government.

Consider the expansion which this principle has enjoyed in our later development. We have since agreed that Congress determines large matters of policy. It leaves interpretation first to those charged with carrying the legislative intention into effect, and ultimately, should question arise, to the courts. The Great Depression of the nineteen-thirties furnished notable examples. The current provision for economic and military aid in the Middle East goes farther. The prodigious growth and complication of the American economy, with corresponding enhancement of the role of government has produced a whole new branch of jurisprudence, administrative law. It is appropriate that scholars of Columbia University, Hamilton's alma mater, have made particular contributions to this field which he helped to open to importance.

Hamilton's inquisitors abused the right, the duty of legislative investigation into official conduct. From the outset, knowing him as Jefferson and Madison did, they could not have believed him culpable. Indulging their political motive, they hampered his useful efforts. Perhaps they did not deserve the complaint of Oliver Wolcott, Sr., that they meant "to make a steady exertion . . . to derange the present system of government." We may credit them with better intent. Call them patriots, but they were also pestiferous in embarrassing the work of a major department. Hamilton met them in the only way possible—by immediate and thorough disclosure of his operations.

Hamilton's vindication of national authority against whisky rebels of western Pennsylvania in 1794 belongs in our story of his political leadership rather than in the account of his fiscal services. The two functions were intimately connected, since the insurrection sprang from refusal to pay the excise on domestic distilled spirits. But the means of redress took on more significance than mere collection of the revenue. Marching 13,000 militia into the country of the recalcitrants proved federal superiority to sectional dissent. Maybe the example had something to do with the effectiveness of President Andrew Jackson's threat to South Carolina nullifiers of customs taxes forty years later. The pity is that after yet another generation secessionists did not bow to national supremacy until vaster retribution was invoked.

It is accurate to speak of Hamilton's principal part in suppressing the whisky rising. He was so credited at the time, with praise or blame depending upon the viewer. He was frequently reproached for interfering in the duties of other departments of the government. Here was a case which, in its origin and course, was within his own responsibility, though correction required military action and afterward involved political remonstrance. It was accidental that when the expedition across the mountains was preparing Hamilton was acting Secretary of War in the absence of General Knox from the capital, but that did not diminish the criticism in Republican quarters of Hamilton's agency.

We may not deal with this vivid occurrence in any detail. As always, there was much to be said on both sides. The crux of the trouble was in the physical and therefore cultural remoteness of the frontiersmen from the eastern seaboard. The Alleghenies, now so swiftly surmounted, were then a formidable barrier. The excise of 1791 was enacted to permit assumption of the state debts. Neither means nor object was approved by the westerners. Their bulky grain, reduced to whisky in ubiquitous farm distilleries, found its market to the eastward where it was lugged by packtrain. The tax must be paid in cash in a country forced to exist by barter. The borderers, individualists by environment, despised the Pennsylvania state excise until it was repealed. They were predisposed to treat the federal duty with similar contempt. This held dangers where whisky was the common drink, rifles hung on every chimney piece, and local autonomy was the popular religion. Scotch-Irish assertiveness hardly needed to be organized in the democratic societies fostered by Citizen Genêt.

Hamilton, solicitous for the revenue but also for harmony and justice, bent to the first storms by modifying the excise to suit the convenience of the distillers. Legislative and administrative adjust-

ments were calculated to meet every reasonable objection. But
these concessions were taken by the insurgents as signals for further
defiance. The house of the inspector of the district was attacked in
force and burned. His subordinates on their errands were shame-
fully abused. Complying distillers had their property wrecked, so
that others were afraid to register. An irregular muster of the
militia, some thousands strong, threatened the log village of Pittsburgh, but the torch was extinguished by kegs of whisky set out by
the inhabitants. Hamilton was bitter against meetings at several
points, particularly Mingo Creek in Washington County, which
gave consistency "to an opposition . . . that threatens the foundations of the government of the Union, unless speedily . . . sub-
dued." Hamilton said these meetings were patronized by influential
persons. He had in mind, among others, H. H. Brackenridge and
Albert Gallatin. The latter was clerk of a meeting which resolved
to obstruct the operation of the law. These Republicans later explained that they attended the meetings in order to quiet the dis-
turbances. Hamilton rightly considered their action equivocal or
worse. The time had come to condemn or condone. Hamilton never
forgave Gallatin. We readily follow the mutual hostility, now en-
gendered, through subsequent political conflicts.

President Washington was persuaded that the resistance must be
put down forthwith. A federal judge having certified that the
courts were powerless, Washington issued a final proclamation,
called out militia from Pennsylvania, Virginia, Maryland, and New
Jersey, and sent ahead commissioners to receive the capitulation
of insurgents. All of these moves were prepared by Hamilton, who
accompanied the punitive expedition. The march was commanded
by Washington as far as Bedford, Pennsylvania, whence the President returned for the session of Congress, placing Governor Henry
Lee in charge. The insurrection melted before this show of federal
force.

But the clash of national authority against regional resistance
reverberated when the President, in his address to Congress, cas-
tigated the "self-created societies" for inflaming opposition to

government. He was thoroughly aroused. His strictures provoked in the House a violent debate in which Federalist and Republican partisans explored the principles involved. How far was free assemblage to be proscribed or protected? The episode split parties as never before. Previous divergence, by comparison, had been tentative. The practical need for funding, assumption, and bank had installed those measures. The cabinet and newspaper quarrel between Hamilton and Jefferson confused personal distaste with political antagonism, and was quieted by the President's remonstrance and Jefferson's early resignation. The rejection of Genêt and issue of the neutrality proclamation claimed a general assent.

Now, however, suppression of regional protest by troops and singling out of local volunteer societies for condemnation awoke the echoes. A new clash was added, destined to ring loud into the future—that of East against West. Hamilton was accused of inflating sporadic disorder into systematic disloyalty. Given the fact of insurrection, he was surely mindful of the salutary results of crushing it. But he was far from seeking the occasion. He tried conciliation, without effect. As Federalist leader he did not invite the spectacle of domestic dissension bearing however faint resemblance to European conflict. The expense burdened the budget. Lastly, as in other instances, he could not have won Washington to a disingenuous purpose.

The Federalists were now victorious, but the Republicans drew strength from defeat. Before entering on next events, which exacerbated differences, we may pause to apply the lesson of the Whisky Insurrection to present events.

We cannot miss the parallel between the refusal of westerners to obey the national law one hundred and sixty years ago and the resistance of parts of the South in face of the desegregation decision of the Supreme Court. In both instances, we find a region in revolt. In both cases it is local geographical, economic, and political peculiarities which provoke disobedience to national mandate. At neither time is enforcement sudden or arbitrary. The whisky excise was modified in amount and in mode of collection.

Washington remonstrated against illegal acts in a proclamation of 1792, which was two years before he felt driven to coercive measures. Likewise, the court, in the desegregation decision, wisely provided time in which offending communities shall bring themselves into conformity.

In both episodes we discover organized opposition on three levels. First, principal spokesmen, persons of education and position, subscribe to defiant resolutions. Second, larger numbers, less identified, form or act through groups of some permanence—the "democratical societies" long ago, and the white citizens' councils now. Third, there is violence, promoted by these organizations or of the *ad hoc* vigilante sort. Further, both sections, while antagonizing national authority, are imploring national assistance. The westerners refused to contribute to the revenue, but they clamored for armed forces to protect them against Indian attack. The southerners in question reject compliance with the court decree but supplicate for flood and drought relief, benefit payments to farmers, and federal assistance to schools. In both examples, the doctrine of states' rights—the South has now revived the term "interposition"—is cried up.

Naturally there are differences between the Whisky Insurrection of our early history and southern contumacy concerning civil rights at present. The area embraced was smaller then—four counties in western Pennsylvania and what was called Ohio County in Virginia. However, less overt opposition had appeared along the frontiers of Maryland and the Carolinas, and, relative to total area and population, we have not much to choose in the two instances. The habit in the South of excluding Negroes from full citizenship is of longer standing than was western animus toward the excise; Jim Crow is older than moonshine, though the latter had already at that early day a respectable history. Some may say that back yonder the national demand was expressed in a statute, accompanied by national enforcement officers, whereas the authority now proceeds in a court decision. But both are equally the law of the land. It will not do to object that an act of Congress is less discretionary than a court opinion. The question of constitutionality of the excise was as loudly raised as is the legality of the recent decision.

No racial problem was involved before, but that is the center of the present controversy. The bugaboo of impending "mongreliza- tion" was not in the earlier picture, but is now proclaimed. I for- bear to stigmatize this last as it deserves. I notice only that, in the first place, it is conjectural. The Supreme Court has not ordered race fusion. If anything, more likelihood of race amalgamation lurks in ignorance and poverty than in education and enlarged opportunity for both whites and Negroes. If the South wants to have white skins on the one hand and black skins on the other, the object will be best achieved by higher economic competence of both groups, with consequent self-esteem of each, and mutual re- spect. It is demonstrated that what produces brown skins is deg- radation and exploitation of Negroes.

President Washington, in the most open fashion, discountenanced regional defiance of national authority. When moral suasion did not serve, and his patience was exhausted, he led troops into the rebel- lious area and compelled obedience to the law. In comparison to that distinguished example, what shall we say of President Eisen- hower's conduct toward refractory southerners? At a similar stage of local disobedience, he has not used his prestige—indeed, has not exercised his constitutional responsibility—to rebuke resistance as Washington did. Washington exerted leadership which Eisenhower has omitted to supply. I wish to be clearly understood. Protest against the court decision has not come to the point calling for federal armed force. May it never reach that pass. The federal civil authority could have been more promptly and more generally em- ployed. In the absence of conspicuous moral support by the Presi- dent of the United States other means to secure compliance with the law will be less effective.

A former justice of the Supreme Court, who was also Secretary of State, has made himself the blatant mouthpiece of Dixie's stand. Southern members of Congress, with a few honorable exceptions, issued a manifesto against the national law. Who shall counter this, save our highest officer speaking in the name of America? Southern university presidents, newspaper editors, and leading writers, again with shining exceptions, have proved obdurate. The timid are following these bold ones, who had their counterparts in the Whisky Insurrection in Brackenridge, Gallatin, Bradford, and more. Will they learn better? May we trust to time for their persuasion? Allow me to say that I am a southerner, born and bred, and I think I know the apologists of sectional mores. They will not yield to national views without coercion. This can be peaceful coercion, but it must proceed from the highest quarter. The Vice-President was sent to West Africa to help celebrate the birth of a new nation of black men, neglecting Negroes in Alabama and Georgia and Florida and Tennessee who are striving for national rights in their own country. The Supreme Court has done its part. Many white southerners, in official and private posts, are doing theirs. The names of Thurgood Marshall and Martin Luther King have flown round the world. One wishes that decided words from the White House were lending resonance to their voices.

The struggle over the Jay treaty takes a central place in the development of parties in our early history. Previous clashes were in different ways subordinate and preparatory to this trial of strength. The funding system, though filled with political implications, was in the realm of the necessary and the technical.

The newspaper duel between Hamilton and Jefferson's proxies bespoke personal as well as political animus, and was so treated by Washington. The attack of Virginians in the House on Hamilton's administration of the Treasury, while noisy, proved abortive. Neutrality wounded French sympathies, but its very name proclaimed detachment, and the policy had the approval of all members of Washington's cabinet. Anti-Federalists must endorse demand for recall of Genêt because he had been grossly presumptuous and Jefferson had too far tolerated his false promises. The Whisky Insurrection, which came next on the boards, was violent disobedience to our own laws, was put down by the President at the head of troops from Southern and Northern states, and in the sequel produced congressional rebuke of the democratic societies.

The Jay treaty, by contrast with precursor acts, was not negative, but positive. It was considered by opponents as ranging us on the side of Britain, our enemy, against France, our political and military ally. It composed our complaints of nonperformance of the peace treaty of 1783, it banished all prospect of belligerency on the side of France in her titanic contest against monarchs. In spite of flagrant British depredations on our shipping, in disregard of established immunities, Jay concluded a commercial treaty such as we did not have with France. Neutrality was one thing, but now it was evident that America's granary was to feed the foes of France.

Actually, the treaty that became the storm center of forces in Congress and the country was Hamilton's far more than Jay's. Hamilton originated the project, munitioned Washington on the desirability of the move, decided him to send Jay as our emissary, helped draw Jay's instructions, and at all stages led the bitter fight for approval of the treaty as concluded. Besides the loyalty in Federalist ranks, individuals conspicuously assisted Hamilton's efforts, particularly Rufus King, soon to be our resident minister to England, and Fisher Ames in the last cast of the dice in the House of Representatives. But Hamilton's solicitude and perseverance were always foremost. The term "father" of this, that, and the other has been overworked. One who was a member of the staff of the monumental *Dictionary of American Biography* relates that it became an editorial rule to eliminate this title after a shoe manufacturer was honored as "the father of the box toe." In the attempt to avoid the forbidden term a publisher was risibly described as "wrapped up in his newspaper." But we must declare that Hamilton was enveloped in the Jay treaty, or he wrapped it up. To appreciate his paternity one must read his early memoranda, his official communications and private letters, and his newspaper essays in elaborate defense of a document which needed all of his intellectual ingenuity and moral commitment for its acceptance.

Here was national leadership which transcended party maneuver, of a high order hardly imitated again until Lincoln's apostleship for union, Wilson's construction of the League of Nations, and Franklin Roosevelt's assault on the Great Depression. The last analogy, in several points of view, may be less apt than the others; in any event, Hamilton was his own "Brain Trust." Procedure since his day has changed. Now the candidate, or important office holder, or national committee chairman is put forward by the party, has a corps of speech-writers, is briefed for pronouncements. In Hamilton's case, he took the position which others chose to follow. While he was not inattentive to party recruitment, management of elections, and legislative votes, he did not so much improve issues as he announced and pressed them to decision.

In the beginning he was fatuous, as were Washington and others, in deploring the very appearance of parties, or factions as they were significantly called. He soon discovered that party strife was bound to be, and he accepted the gage of battle. In subsequent American habit we have allowed party to dim principle. At least our expectation is that only in party combat shall we define principle. The case with Hamilton was different. Aroused to purpose, party —his own or another's—played a minor role in his calculation. He addressed himself to influential individuals, generally but not always of his persuasion, and when his plan was in train he appealed to public opinion. I know the canniness, or perhaps cynicism, which regards all statesmen as politicians, and refuses to divest them of party motive. Only one who depicts Washington is allowed to impute purer prompting. An accurate view of Hamilton, when at his best, must give him similar accolade. It is true that, naturally enough, he became increasingly party-conscious, and attempted to be, indeed, the manipulator of a cadre within the ranks of the Federalists.

In the controversy over Jay's treaty he was pleading in the

national interest. In our infant state our continued prosperity demanded peace. In our defenseless condition war would impose unsupportable burdens, desolation of the frontiers, and perhaps internal revolution. "We ought to be wise enough to see that this is not a time for trying our strength." We must buy time, ten or a dozen years, until our "embrio of a great empire" could mature and "take a higher and more imposing tone." He declared accurately that "opposers of the treaty . . . have put invention on the rack, to accumulate charges against it . . . without regard even to plausibility." The "good sense of the people must be relied upon" to "disappoint those who are . . . making experiments upon their credulity, . . . treating them as children, . . . to lead them blindfold. . . ."

Hamilton was respecting democracy, not exploiting it. He rested in the hope "that it will be sufficient for the people's conviction to give solid answers to all such objections as have the semblance of reason . . ." As Lodge has observed, Hamilton had no art for ward politics, and insofar was ill fitted to build a political machine. By choosing the state and oftener the national forum, and depending on argument to determine principal issues, he made the Federalists, not by design, too much a one-man party. This later led to party dissension and decline. Aside from this defect, danger lurked in the bony structure, as it were, of the Federalists. The party was inspired by the relatively few of possessions and prudent patriotism. Hamilton called them "that description of men which are in every society the only firm supporters of government." These, eager for harmony, might lapse into coercion to insure safety. Centralized authority and insistence on order may readily, in time of crisis, degenerate into attempted dictatorship. Of course this is the derogation of democracy.

On the other hand, the party of contrary stamp, resting on broad popular appeal, may debase democracy if its leaders adroitly seize "a favorable moment to furorize the public opinion." Which holds more risks for a free society is a question. Fortunately in America we have escaped the ultimate machinations of either the self-righteous few or the deluded many. On the whole we have had more taste of the perils of the latter. To this extent we may confide in Hamilton's mortal hatred of the demagogue. The authoritarian has at least the virtue of acknowledging responsibility. The inflamer of popular passions dodges, in the name of democracy, the reproach which belongs to him. Hamilton as a party leader, profoundly wishing the benefit of the people, and not stooping to flattery, was constantly sensitive to fraudulent declaimers.

President and Senate ratified the treaty with the exception of one completely ineligible article. But Republican leaders wanted the House of Representatives to be included with President and Senate in the treaty-making power where the House was called upon for funds to carry the engagement into effect. For this purpose, after stormy debate the House passed resolutions requesting Washington to submit Jay's instructions and additional documents relating to the negotiations. Hamilton gave the President full support in the decision that this application must be refused. Hamilton more than others had all along defended the executive function. He had acted on the assumption that a treaty, approved by the President with the advice and consent of the Senate, became the law of the land, and the House was bound to carry out its provisions. In the end the House made the required appropriations, but declared its possession of discretionary authority to give or withhold funds contemplated in a treaty. Left in this equivocal state, the constitutional contest recurred on later occasions.

One asks what would be Hamilton's position on the proposed (Bricker) constitutional amendment including the House with President and Senate in the power to make treaties and agreements with foreign nations or international organizations. Any answer—of course speculative at best—must take account of changes in our world relations and in our domestic polity. Our agreements are no more with this or that nation, but with blocs of allies or potential allies. Our engagements are not to do this and abstain from that, but result in programs of action developing over indefinite periods. These programs have consequences for our internal economy, for better or worse. Formal treaties, punctuated in time, are superseded by executive commitments, less specific but more momentous in their operation. In the process the House, as the popular branch of our legislature, has been drawn into closer cooperation with Senate and President in the design and administration of foreign policy. Our prospect, vis-à-vis a great part of the world supposed to be hostile, has become the concern, almost the obsession of the ordinary citizen in a fashion never so true before. Our external obligations force us into an extension of national authority at home. In this situation local American interests, states' rights, cannot enjoy a negative on national, or international, policy. They cannot be effectually protected by the courts. They may be consulted only, but how, unless Congress has a voice, with President and the upper house, in formulating and concluding foreign undertakings.

I hazard the guess that Hamilton would favor Senator Bricker's proposal, or something to similar purpose. This would be in spite of his emphasis upon executive authority. His overweening desire was for national unity, strength, and responsibility. He always showed a solicitude for the House of Representatives, standing for the republican principle. His care for the Senate was technical and subordinate. Perhaps he would recognize that the federal courts, whose role he stressed, cannot serve, in the present context, by defending the Constitution as a written document. Perhaps judicial review would prove too inert by nature. Hamilton was supremely sensible to the dynamic character of our country, expressing itself by virtue of implied powers. Under present exigencies, representative government may be better preserved by cooperation than by separation of powers within our constitutional system.

Whether this needs to be stated in an amendment, or should rather be accepted as a rule of practice is a connected but distinct question. The procedure proposed—that is, incorporation of Congress in the making as well as the execution of foreign policy—commends itself because our foreign contracts now typically commit us to overseas subsidies, prodigious and continuing. Appropriations did not bulk anywhere near so large in our international engagements before World War II. A high proportion of what we grant—too high—is for military aid. This brings these agreements further into the bailiwick of the House. Drawing undeveloped countries to our side, equipping them with armaments, and establishing bases on their soil certainly looks to the event of war. The Eisenhower plan for swift use of United States troops in the Middle East, if need arises, on presidential order, is a further trenching on the function of Congress. Maybe it confirms the notion that Hamilton would approve frank inclusion of the House of Representatives in the shaping of foreign agreements which so impinge on war.

Hamilton's promotion and defense of the Jay treaty, finished in 1795, was high tide of his public performance and influence. After that his wisdom and success declined. He was without official responsibility, except for the brief period, 1798–1800 when, as Inspector-General, he was organizing the provisional army to meet expected attack by France. He was best in helping to drive the car of state. Then he was strong, courageous, but prudent. As an outrider he departed from the true road. It is instructive, but sad, to follow the events of the last years of his life. They embrace a long denouement in which his magnificent powers were often misapplied. His old vigor remained—if anything, was laid under more demands than ever—but he directed it into wrong tracks. The degree of restraint that he had exercised earlier forsook him. On the inside, looking out he had preserved a sense of fitness, but now, on the outside and looking in he became arbitrary. He was superb in creation, but intolerant as a critic. This observation applies to his conduct on several occasions that we shall mention. Circumstantial excuses may be found. He was driving himself beyond limits, tending his busy law practice while as deeply immersed in public affairs as a private citizen could be. His health suffered. Near the end of the period he had the double tragedy of the death of his eldest son, Philip, in a duel, and the lapse of his eldest daughter, Angelica, into a mental disorder from which she never recovered. But the trouble lay deeper, in the failure of his own mind and judgment to adapt to changes taking place in the country.

In 1797 James Monroe had been recalled from his post of minister to France, and the Federalists were heaping retribution on his head for having embraced Jacobins and sheltered Tom Paine. Monroe smarted under these attacks. James T. Callender, a Republican pamphleteer, took up cudgels for Monroe by raking up an old but hitherto unpublished slander against Hamilton. He exhibited documents purporting to show that Hamilton had been guilty of collusive speculation while at the head of the Treasury. He suggested that to escape these proofs Hamilton concocted an unlikely and shameful story of an illicit love-affair. This revival of accusation went back almost five years to December, 1792. At that time Senator Monroe and Congressmen Venable and Frederick Muhlenburg had confronted Hamilton with evidence which they suspected impugned his behavior in office. He invited them to a conference at his home, when he would convince them that their insinuations were groundless. He took the precaution of having Wolcott, his trusted friend and associate, present as witness. Hamilton laid out further correspondence and receipts which showed that his dealings with James Reynolds and Jacob Clingman, a couple of miscreants who had been the false informers, grew out of a liaison with Mrs. Reynolds, which had been recently terminated. The three inquisitors thereat professed themselves satisfied of the Secretary's innocence of official malfeasance, and withdrew under the obligation to bury the incident in oblivion.

When the aspersion was resuscitated, in the most twisted form, by Callender, Hamilton taxed the trio of political foes to disavow the dishonorable disclosure. Venable and Muhlenburg cleared themselves, but Monroe admitted that he had listened to fresh accusations, and Hamilton fixed on him the disclosure to Callender. (The fact is unquestionable that the papers were conveyed to Callender by John Beckley, a minor Virginia politician, and probably without Monroe's knowledge.) Monroe had no stomach for a duel with Hamilton. But that would have solved nothing anyhow. How should Hamilton meet Callender's pretended exposures? He could frown them down in silent disdain, which his friends thought proper. But he was so sensitive of his official honor that he resolved to vindicate it by declaring his private misconduct with Maria Reynolds. This he did in a long pamphlet which omitted no particular of a sordid affair complete with blackmail by the husband. Rarely has honest confession paid off more handsomely. His family was loyal, and his political enemies who mattered sunk his lesser error in his greater merit. Still, it had been a messy business, and recurrent mean reproaches could be more easily despised than dismissed.

French seizures of our ships were matched by affront to the nation when a bribe was demanded of our special envoys seeking accommodation. President Adams was resentful enough to want to prepare us for our defense on land and at sea. Hamilton dropped his law practice to take on the task of organizing our resistance. He was too eager to be Inspector-General and first in command under Washington. To force this preference he hurt the pride of General Knox, who had the better claim from old rank and service, and he incurred the further distaste of Adams. Hamilton's motives were as much domestic as in the field of foreign relations. He wanted to press the advantage against the Republicans, apologists of France, who were embarrassed in proportion to America's indignation. In the beginning he drew back at the Alien and Sedition acts, counseling "let us not erect a tyranny." But as events matured he too far assented in their operation. The answer of beleaguered political opponents, Jefferson and Madison, in the Kentucky and Virginia resolutions opened to Hamilton, if anything more were needed, the full length of states' rights to which they would go.

Hamilton's furious preparation against France embraced peripheral projects of expeditions against Spanish Louisiana and Florida and, with possible British help, revolutionary liberation of Latin America. But all were paper plans, contingent on French behavior.

Hamilton did not want war, foreign or civil. However, he did not let one hand know what the other did. The crisis was as much in his own fears and hatreds as in the relations of the two countries. Thus it came that when Adams made a sudden aboutface and composed matters with the Directory, Hamilton was set back on his heels. The defense he had marshaled must be disbanded, for there was no foe. Still, he knew and declared this was a good result. He had helped produce peace.

In the spring of 1800 the Federalists were in a panic. It was certain that the New York legislature, newly elected, would be controlled by the anti's. This legislature would choose Republican electors, which would give the Presidency to Jefferson. In his alarm Hamilton made a discreditable proposal to Governor Jay. It was that the old legislature, still in office, be called in special session to change the law so that electors would be chosen by the people in districts. This would yield Federalist electors and prevent the victory of Jefferson. Dwelling on the subversive designs of the anti's, Hamilton persuaded himself that the Federalists could not be squeamish. The ends—"the great cause of social order"—justified the means. This was self-deception. What he urged was fraudulent, degrading, even venal. He would defeat the purpose of the whole people by an illicit trick in one state. This impugned his honor and his national principle.

Governor Jay summarily rejected the unworthy device. Hamilton had touched low point in political morality. His dodge is emphasized because it was uncharacteristic of him.

Several years before, Hamilton had rejected just such an illegitimate expedient. This was in 1792, when Jay, as the Federalists believed, had been counted out of his election to the New York governorship by Clinton's board of canvassers. "To rejudge the decision of the canvassers by a convention," he wrote King, "has to me too much the appearance of reversing the sentence of a court by a legislative decree. . . . I do not feel it right . . . to attempt to reverse the decision by any means not known to the

Constitution or laws." Moreover, he reflected, such a precedent, at a future day, might be used by their enemies.

Hamilton's effort in 1800 to defeat the election of Jefferson betrayed his loss of balance, his wild resort to any means to serve his aim. This was his confession of unfitness for further party leadership. Aside from the swelling strength of the Republicans, he was finished. Fortunately, as we shall see, he righted himself before it was too late for his reputation. He recovered from his frenzy in time to vindicate his patriotism.

However, before he collected himself he made a capital misplay. "In a very belligerent humor," as he confided to Wolcott, he published, in the midst of the presidential campaign of 1800, a full-scale attack on John Adams, the titular head of the Federalist party. Since the days of the Revolution he had had suspicions of Adams's wisdom. When Washington retired, Hamilton had supported Adams equally with Thomas Pinckney for the presidency. Some electors did not share Hamilton's secret hope that Pinckney would win, threw away votes, and Jefferson became vice-president. Four years later Hamilton had moved on to disgust with Adams's capricious egotism. "I will never more be responsible for him," Hamilton declared, "by my direct support, even though the consequence should be the election of *Jefferson*." The reasons are not far to seek. Ironically, Hamilton had come to share some of the vacillation of which he accused Adams. Despite disclaimer, he was personally piqued with Adams, who behind Hamilton's back had called him pro-British. Adams, in a flash of revelation, had dismissed cabinet ministers—Pickering and McHenry—who had steadily been Hamilton's allies or instruments in executive policy. The collapse of the provisional army had left Hamilton temporarily in a void.

Hamilton's main effort in the assault on Adams was to prefer Charles Cotesworth Pinckney for the presidency. This required argument with the middling Federalists, who were loyal to Adams. But Hamilton washed the party's dirty linen in public. He was as deliberate as he was wrong-headed. He knew and said beforehand that his pamphlet would be common property in the national contest. It was a damaging piece of business. Every paragraph was a pull on the rope that rang the knell of the Federalists.

Hamilton was prepared for defeat. But he made it defeat with honor. When Jefferson and Burr were tied at the top of the poll, Hamilton discountenanced Federalist bargaining with Burr.

Years earlier, he had held the same principles. He wrote Washington in 1792 that Federalist factionalists ought not to seek to buy power by embracing Republican enemies. This could only serve individual ambition. He profoundly disagreed with Jefferson's principles, but he believed that Burr had no principle but personal ambition, which he would gratify to the country's ruin. In letters to leading Federalists, and surely in exhortation otherwise, he exerted himself mightily to warn his party away from Burr, though at the expense of elevating Jefferson to the presidency. He could not have been more explicit or morally earnest. He took high ground of pleading for "lasting prosperity and glory to the country," "to unite liberty with strength." For the Federalists to support Burr would be "a fatal mistake," since "he has but one principle— to *get power* by *any* means and to *keep* it by *all* means." Burr would court "war and disorder, or . . . a sale to a foreign power, or . . . great speculation." Admonishing Gouverneur Morris, Hamilton left no doubt of the price he was prepared to pay to block Burr: "If there be a man in the world I ought to hate, it is Jefferson. With Burr I have always been personally well. But the public good must be paramount to every personal consideration." And again to James A. Bayard: "To contribute to the disappointment and mortification of Mr. J., would be, on my part, only to retaliate for unequivocal proofs of enmity; but in a case like this, it would be base to listen to personal considerations." John Rutledge could not "render a greater service to his country than by exerting . . . influence to counteract the . . . impure idea of raising Mr. Burr to the chief magistracy." To James Ross: "Let the Federalists vote for Jefferson," improving the opportunity to obtain assurances from him that public credit, support of the navy, and *bona fide* neutrality would be preserved. Jefferson had superior character and ability. In helping to elevate Jefferson to first place, Hamilton rediscovered his own nobility.

It was not the last time. In 1804 Burr, disgruntled, sought the governorship of New York with Federalist assistance. Hamilton blocked him with the freest aspersions on his public and private character. Morgan Lewis, the Republican candidate, was elected.

This was the signal for Hamilton's exit. His remarkable part in the founding of the nation was played out. He could not have rescued the Federalist party. The previous decade had shown as much. Maybe, in the strange way it has, fortune sped Burr's bullet in the duel. Hamilton died in a last service to the Union. That had always been his passion.

IN SUMMARY

$\mathscr{T}$RYING to acquaint oneself with Alexander Hamilton, man and statesman, one is mindful of his intelligence and courage, and the commitment of all his faculties to the service of the public. These qualities informed every episode of his career. In assessing the record of his life one is safer in a presupposition in his favor because of his power of thought and his moral integrity. His distinction is compounded of these merits—insight, honorable intent, and unselfish devotion. Failings, even follies he had, and these detracted from his virtues, though not so much from his accomplishments. His mistakes of judgment argue the overtaxing of his remarkable capacities. His eager mind and nervous enegry made unreasonable demands on his physical strength, which, even so, bore the burden better than he had a right to expect.

His ability to focus, to keep values in proportion, declined in the last years. He had burned the candle at both ends. He did not practice his former self-discipline. Ironically, the age of his wisdom was earlier rather than later. Elements of extravagance entered. His animosities became untempered, embittered. But this falling off was not complete nor continuous. He could catch himself and rise to his old heights. His final choice to see his Federalists yield to Jefferson rather than compound with Aaron Burr was a glory. Triumph wrapped his tragedy.

His was a life of superlatives, with little of the commonplace. One does not forget the aphorism that genius is the capacity for taking pains. Hamilton was indefatigible. None of his work was careless, or *pro forma*. All had substance, coherence, and finish. Another of excellent parts, with his industry, could have produced the technical features of his Treasury reports. His virtue was over and above this proficiency. It sprang from imagination and rare dedication that made the difference between the good and the splendid. He perceived the potentialities of America. He saw the promise of the future and imported it into his proposals. This enabled him to turn debt into credit, minus into plus.

It is artificial to separate Hamilton's economic expedients from his political resourcefulness. The two were blended in his purpose and method. This was inevitable while the country was in its infancy. His claims as an economist, which are high, have been blurred by his constant recourse to political means. This is not to be regretted. His concern was nothing less than the making of a nation.

Few of the founding fathers have become obsolete. They are not patriotic monuments; they live in influence in our America. The penchant of some was for the dignity of man. Others were absorbed in framing institutions for the prosperity of society. With conflicts between them along the way, their efforts meshed. Hamilton is among the most modern of that prophetic company. Our union, security, and productivity bear out his forecast. We could speak of particulars in national development, political and economic, which are fruits of his hopes and work. Among the first lines he ever wrote is the outburst, "my ambition is prevalent." That was in a distant island. In the continent which received him it is still so.

The Man in His Own Words

This letter, my very dear Eliza, will
not be delivered to you, unless I shall first
have terminated my earthly career; to begin, as
I humbly hope from redeeming grace and divine
mercy, a happy immortality.

If it had been possible for me
to have avoided the interview, my love for
you and my precious children would have been alone a
decisive motive — But it was not possible,
without sacrifices which would have rendered
me unworthy of your esteem. I need not tell you
of the pangs I feel, from the idea of quitting
you and exposing you to the anguish which
I know you would feel. Nor could I dwell
on the topic lest it should unman me.

The consolations of Religion,
my beloved, can alone support you; and
these you have a right to enjoy. Fly to
the bosom of your God and be comforted.
With my last idea I shall cherish the sweet
hope of meeting you in a better world.

Adieu best of wives and best
of Women. Embrace all my darling Children
for me.

ever yours
A H

July 4. 1804

93353

Mrs Hamilton

In this feeling farewell to his wife Hamilton acknowledges the necessity for even the molder of public opinion to bow to views and customs which he could not change. The last—and fatal—instance of his conformity was his acceptance of the demands of the duel.

The following letters have been chosen to reveal Hamilton the man rather than the statesman. They do something to correct the temptation, more noticeable as we retreat from his lifetime, to know him as a public figure, not as a person. In Hamilton's case this tendency to neglect, or erase, his human qualities is especially strong. Throughout his relatively short career he gave himself unstintingly to official assignments and, beyond the call of duty, to obligations of a citizen. Little leisure remained for indulgence in avocations, for cultivating literature and the arts, and none for pleasurable travel, or the introspections of a diary. Such bypaths, had he trod them, would have afforded us a fuller record of his private thoughts and emotions.

Even so, we may recapture him as precocious youngster in the West Indies, as zealous and proud military aide to Washington, as friend, lover, husband, and father. We see him in the end revolving the claims of his family and his conscience against his commitment as political leader. From the whole comes the surprise that he was more than a thinking machine and a driving force. This man of decision and will was also solicitous for others, gifted with charm as well as self-confidence, had his moments of humility and frank apology.

Several of the letters are here printed for the first time. All, except in a few cases where the originals are not available, reproduce Hamilton's spelling, punctuation, and the like, with only minimal editing where modern usage appears to aid the reader.

TO EDWARD STEVENS

The earliest letter of Alexander Hamilton which has been preserved is that to Edward Stevens, about his own age, who had been sent from the island of St. Croix to the Continent for schooling. Alexander had received kindnesses from Edward's father, who was on his way to visit his son. The letter (the original has been identified by the editors of the Papers of Alexander Hamilton), was written when Alexander was two months short of fifteen years old, if we accept January 11, 1755 (not 1757) as the date of his birth. Even so, it proclaims his ambition which, Washington testified, was "of that *laudable kind, which prompts a man to excel in whatever he takes in hand.*" Alexander and Edward remained friends for life; Dr. Stevens cured Hamilton of yellow fever in the Philadelphia epidemic of 1793.

St. Croix Novemr 11 1769

Dear Edward

This just serves to acknowledge receipt of yours per Cap Lowndes which was delivered me yesterday, the truth of Cap Lightbowen & Lowndes information is now verifyd by the presence of your Father and Sister for whose safe arrival I Pray, and that they may convey that satisfaction to your soul that must naturally flow from the sight of absent Friends in health, and shall for news this way refer you to them, as to what you say respecting your having soon the happiness of seeing us all, I wish, for an accomplishment of your hopes provided they are Concomitant with your welfare, otherwise not, tho doubt whether I shall be Present or not, for to confess my weakness, Ned, my Ambition is prevalent. That I contemn the grov'ling condition of a Clerk or the like, to which my Fortune &c condemns me and would willingly risk my life though not my Character to exalt my station, I'm confident, Ned that my Youth excludes me from any hopes of immediate Perferment, nor do I desire it, but I mean to prepare the way for futurity, I'm no Philosopher you see and may be justly said to Build Castles in the Air, my Folly makes me ashamed and beg youll conceal it, yet Neddy we have seen such schemes successful when the Projector is Constant. I shall Conclude saying I wish there was a war.

   I am

      dr Edward

                     yours

                                Alex Hamilton

PS I this moment received yours by William Smith and am pleased to see you Give such Close Application to Study.

EARLY LETTERS FROM ST. CROIX

The following six letters, written by Hamilton, when about seventeen, from Nicholas Cruger's store in St. Croix, are now published for the first time. Cruger had gone to New York for his health, leaving Alexander in charge of his considerable affairs. The maturity and competence with which the youth discharged his responsibility provoke admiration. Cruger, appreciative of the efforts of his proxy, doubtless contributed to send him to the Continent for an education.

Mr. Nicholas Cruger   St. Croix Novem. 12 177[1]
Dr Sir
per Lowndes

   I send you herewith Copies of my Letter's per Codwise & Cunningham, since which nothing has occurd worth writing. Markets are just the same excepting in the price of Butter which is now reduced to 15 & 16 per a firkin. Your Philadelphia flour is realy very bad being of a most swarthy complexion & withal very untractable; the Bakers complain that they cannot by any means get it to rise. Wherefore & in consideration of the quantity of flour at Market and the little demand for it I have some thought not to refuse 8½ from any good person that will give it—taking 40 or 50 Barrels. Upon opening several barrels I have observ'd a kind of Worm very common in flour about the surface—which is an indication of Age. It could not have been very new when twas shipd and for all these reasons I conceive it highly necessary to lessen the price or probably I may be oblig'd in the end to sell it at a much greater disadvantage. At 8½ you will gain better than 10 rys per bbl which is not so bad. York flour of 1.3 is gladly sold by every body at 8p at retail & a grea[t] part of your Philadelphia weighs but little more so that 8½ by the quantity is more than a proportionable price for the difference of weight.

There is still on hand about 290 barrels. All Lightbo[u]rns is sold at 9 & near all your Fathers p Draper at 8 ps. As to bread I have sold very little. I dont know what to think of it.

The matter between Mr. Heyliger & Mr. Mahan is still unsettled. M Bartram French who was to have been arbitrator for the former is at portoricco and he pretends he can get no one else to supply his place. Mr. French is minutely expected & it is to be hopd that when he arrives there will be a settlement.

No appearance of the Thunderbolt nor no News from Curracoa. I am with unfeigned Regard—Dear Sir

Your very Hum Serv

St Croix Novembr 27. 177[1]

Mess[rs] Jacob Walton & J. H. Cruger
Gentlemen

I have now the pleasure to acknowledge the receipt of your favour dated October the 19th by Sloop Thunderbolt which arrived here on Wednesday Afternoon the 16th Instant—and on the Saturday morning following—I cleard her out and gave the Captain his dispatches for Curracoa, but he could not sail till the morning after. She landed here only

23 Hhds Indian Meal
6469 Staves—
20 bbls Apples
300 Boards Inch & half
&—21 Kegs Bread——
& 646. Ropes onions

All the rest of her Cargo (I think) must turn out better at Curracoa than here—or at any rate not worse. Could I have landed
the super fine Flour conveniently and without detention I should
have done it—but the Captain told me—it was stow'd so promiscu-
ously that to get at it, would require some time. Wherefore I have
sent it down to take its chance with the rest of the Cargo, there
being not a moment of time to spare—our Crops are so forward.
As to the 2 Hhds Indian meal, the kegs of Water Bread, the few
Staves and, I may add, the Boards, that were sent down rather
improperly. They could not be got at or I should have landed
them.

The price of common N Y flour here is 7½ & 8ps. & I fancy it
cant well be less at Curracoa. There has been large quantitys of
Rye Meal—brought here lately from Copenhagen—barrels weigh-
ing 250 Nt have been sold at 3½ & 4 ps. Tis true the quality is
somewhat inferior to that of New york, but the difference of
Weight is adequate to the inferiority of Quality—so that New
York Rye Meal would not fetch above 4 ps per barrel—at most—
& must at least be worth as much below.

This is nearly the case with every other Article sent down—
which youll observe per Inclosd price Current. I have desird Mr.
Teleman Cruger to return the Staves by the Sloop if they will
be no incumbrance to her and to give the 2Hhds containing the
Indian Meal to Capt Newton for Water Casks. I supplied him with
20 here but he thought he should want a few more. I am selling the
Indian Meal at 23 ps per Hhd & expect £10 per thousand for the
Staves (all for Crop pay). The Apples were in every respect very
indifferent. The greatest part of them I sold at 20 rys & the rest at
12. Four Rys per piece is the price of the Boards and per 2 ps.
of the kegs of Water Bread. As to the Onions I was glad to get rid
of them altogether for 40 ps.

A large Sloop with 70 Mules from the Main arrivd two days
ago. The terms of Sale—Joes down—which gives me high hopes
that he will be oblig'd to go further—Cash of all kinds being very
scarce here. Even Danish bits are not to be had much less Joes.

The Captain talks largely of Dangers & difficultys upon the Coast—but no doubt exaggerates a good deal [by way of stimulation].

Excepting this one circumstance (a little unfavourable) every thing has a very promising aspect with regard to the price of Mules this Season & I hope will continue so. But I imagine we are rather too late for Cargoes. This I shall be better able to judge of by and by.

Concerning your Tea—you may depend I shall be strictly observant of your directions.

And conclusively I beg leave to assure you Gentlemen that I gave the Sloop Thunderbolt all the dispatch I could from here. The Articles landed from on Board of her tho triffling were very tedious and always take up more time than other things.

Mr. Nicho. Cruger   St Croix Jan 10th [1772]
via Merryland & Philadelphia
Dear Sir

Your agreeable Letters of the 12 and 20th Ultimo were yesterday handed me [by] Mr Lynsen and Capt Gibb, who arrivd within a few hours of each other. Nothing cou'd be more pleasing to me than to hear of the reestablishment of your Health, and I sincerely wish you a permanent possession of that invaluable blessing.

The 101 barrils superfine Flour from Philladilphia are just landed, about 40 of which I have already sold at 11½ ps per bbl but as tis probable there will be much less imported than I expected I intend to insist on 12 for the rest. Capt Napper is arrivd and dld [declared] every thing agreeable to his Bill Lading. He landed all at the Westend. The Beer I beg'd Mr. Herbert to sell there. The plate Stockings &c. are deposited in Miss Nancy DiNullys hands—and the cheeses in Number 4 were disposed of thus two Mr. Beekman and self kept and the other two I sent on to Mrs. De Nully.

I called upon Mr Heyns to Day with the Bill on Capt Suntis but he was at the Westend so that I can say nothing of that matter. (Mr Heyns I am told is Capt Hunters Attorney)

Capt Gibbs is landing as fast as possible and you may depend I will give him all the dispatch in my power but I will not undertake to determine precisely when he will Sail as he tells me his Cargo is stow'd very inconveniently and the St Croix part of it rather undermost. If so he will be detained longer than cou'd otherwise be expected. His Cargo will turn out pritty well. Lumber is high £18 per M—and most of the other Articles in Demand enough. But as I am a good deal hurried just now I beg youll accept this instead of a more minute detail of these matters which I shall send by the Next conveyance. I have not time to write your Father.

I shall do as you desire concerning the Brig Nancys Accounts.

Capt Wells Cargo consisted of Lumber Spermac[eti]. Candles Codfish and Ale Wives. All the Hoops he brought were sold imediately to Mr Bignall at 70 ps per M. and the Spermaceta Candles to differnt persons at 6 rys per 11. We are selling the Codfish at ps. 6½ per Ct and the Ale Wives at 5 and 6 ps per barrill. He will return in about 10 Days with Sugar and a few Bales of Cotton.

I have not seen Mr Kortright yet to know the particulars of your contract about the Lumber but I make no doubt it will turn out to your wish. I shall provide for it.

When an Opportunity offers I shall do as you desire about the Fustick—Believe me Sir I dun as hard as is proper. The tea is not yet arrived but Ill keep it when it dose in Store as you Direct.

I minutely expect Capt Newton from the Main and I think we need not fear geting a good price for his Mules when he arrives. I wrote you fully the 27th Novemr Via St Thomas concerning him and shou'd now send Copies but for my hurry as before mention'd. It is strange I have never receiv'd a line from Curracoa.

I return you many thanks for the Apples you were so kind as to send me and shall carefully deliver the little complimentary articles when landed to the respective persons.

This is all I have time to say now and if I have neglected any thing material I beg youll excuse it being with the closest attention to your Interest and most Sincere regard

Dear Sir

Your most Obdt Servt

Alexander Hamilton

I shall provide the Rum and
Sugar for Capt Gibb.
the price of Rum now is 2/9

Capt William Newton   St Croix Febru 1. 1771 [2]

Proceed immediately with the Sloop Thunderbolt to Curracoa— & deliver the articles you have on Board agreeable to Bill—Lading. Follow Mr Telleman Crugers directions in every Respect thenceforward & I trust I may rely on you to perform your part with all possible diligence & dispatch. Reflect continually on the unfortunate Voyage you have just made and endeavour to make up for the considerable loss therefrom accruing to your Owners. Lay in at least a Months supply for your Mules. Let me beg that if Mr T. Cruger does not furnish the Vessell with 4 Guns—youll do it yourself before you go to the Main—I mean hire them before you go & leave them when you return, paying the Hire which you shall be repaid here. This is all I think needful to say so I wish you a good passage & am

Your Obdt Serv

for N Cruger

A Hamilton

Teleman Cruger Esqr.   St Croix Febru 1771 [2]
Sir

Two days ago Capt Newton delivered me your favour without date & 41 Mules in such order that I have been oblig'd to send all of them to pasture—and of which I expect at least a third will die. The highest offer made me for 20 of the best was 70 ps—whereas if they had been in good order I could readily have obtaind £40 round—which I all along entertaind the most sanguine hopes of. Thus you see how unfortunate the Thunderbolts first Voyage has been. But we must try a second time. Accordingly I have put on Board her some Codfish, Rum & Bread as per. Inclosd Bill Lading & wish them to a good Market.

Capt Newton is to supply himself with Grass on his way down & I must beg the favour of you by all means to buy or hire him a few Guns which is agreeable to Mr. Crugers directions to me. I should do it here if it were possible but there are none to be had upon any terms whatever & it would be undoubtedly a great pity that such a Vessell should be lost for the want of them. To hire would be preferable—which Capt Newton tells me may be done at 20 ps per Month for a p.[air].

It is thought by Judges that the Sloop Thunderbolt ought to carry 60 Mules. If you think so—please to desire the Capt to do it. I have mentioned it to him—but he insists that 48 are as many as she can conveniently hold. The more she brings the better. But I do not pretend to be a Judge of the matter & therefore leave it to you.* Please to send by the Sloops return a full state of accounts between you & Mr. Cruger that I may enter all things properly.

---

* But Without the utmost dispatch her second Voyage may miscarry like the first.

Mr. Nicholas Cruger   St Croix February 24 177[2]
Dr. Sir
per Lightbourn

Herewith you have duplicate of my two last Letters of the 27 November & 10th Ulto. and I now congratulate myself upon the pleasure of addressing you again—but am sorry I shall be obligd to communicate some dissatisfactory occurrencies.

Your Sloop Thunderbolt arrivd here the 29th of the preceding Month with 41 More Skeletons. A worse parcel of Mules never was seen she took in at first 48 & lost 7 on the passage. I sent all that were able to walk to pasture, in Number 33. The other 8 could hardly stand for 2 Minutes together & in spite of the greatest care 4 of them are now in Limbo. The Surviving 4 I think are out of Danger—and shall likewise be shortly sent to pasture. I refusd two great offers made me upon their first landing to Wit 70 ps. a head for the Choice of 20—and 15 ps. a Head for the abovementiond Invalids—which may give you a proper idea of the condition they were in. Taking this along with it—that if they had been such as we had reason to hope they would be I could with pleasure have had £40 round. So unfortunate has the Voyage been—However [—] by sending them to pasture I expect to get £100 round for those now alive. 17 are already gone at that price and as they recruit fast the rest I hope will soon go at the same—I pay 2 ps. a Head Montly for pasturage. The Sloop was 27 days on her passage from the Main. Not for want of swiftness [—] for tis now known she Sails well—but from continual Calms & the little wind she had was quite against her. Capt Newton seemd to be much concernd at his Ill luck tho I believe he had done all in his power to make the voyage successful. But no Man can command the Winds. The Mules were pretty well chosen & had been once a good parcel. I receivd only a few lines from your Brother. No Sales nor anything else; he excusd himself being Sick. I desird him as directed to furnish the Sloop with a few Guns but she went intirely defence-less to the Main—nothwithstanding several Vessells had been obligd to put back to get out of the way of the Launches with which the Coast swarms. When Capt Newton urgd him to hire a few Guns for the Sloop He replied to this effect—that I only had mentiond the matter to him—but that you had never said a word about it. This last time I mentiond it again & begd the Captain to hire 4 Guns himself if your Brother did not which he has promisd to do. The Expence will not be above 15. or 20 ps.—and one escape may not be followd by a second, neither do I see any reason to run the risque of it. I sent down on your account 10 Hhds Codfish, 8 Hhds Rum, 40 Philad. barrels & 8 Teirces Bread. The Rum Cost 2/7½ & is worth 5 bits a Gallon at Curacoa. I believe those Articles will answer pretty well.

Upon application to Mr Heyns I found I had been misinformd & that Mr Hunter has no Attorney here—whereupon I wrote him a Letter to St Thomas & have sent him three Copys of the Same without receiving any answer. Mr. Ringger is here and is going over in a day or two. I intend to give him a Letter & beg hell ask for an answer and send it over. I am a good deal surprisd at Capt Hunters Silence.

Brig Nancys Accounts are inclosd. The Tea is arrivd. It Cost 20¼ Sti—but there is a discount of 4 ps. for prompt payment. I shall send Copy of the Invoice etc. to Mess[rs] Walton & Cruger. The Lumber you contracted for is arrivd & I am a good deal puzzled to fulfil your engagements, it is rather early you know to receivd [receive it] & Cash is scarce—Mr Beekman would Ship on freight —which would ease the matter but he can receive none yet. However I must manage some how or other. It would be a pity to pay dead freight.

As to introducing Wine, it depends upon Circumstances. There is none here at present and if yours could be brought while the scarcity continues it would not be difficult to obtain permission to land it. Other-wise it will be impracticable—unless our General who is momently expected should bring any new indulgence concerning that article. But the whole is a chance.

Many changes of Officers are talkd of in particular tis said Judge Sevel will be superceded by Jeger the informer & the Collector by the present Comptroler—which is all that occurs to me now. Therefore Ill conclude wishing you safe passage out. I am

   Sir

Your Obdt Serv

AH

TO WILLIAM HAMILTON

The unusually autobiographical letter below was to the Laird of Grange, in Ayrshire, Scotland, who was Alexander Hamilton's first cousin. Grange was the ancestral home, where Alexander's father, James Hamilton, had grown up.

Albany, State of New York
May the 2d. 1797

My Dear Sir

Some days since I received with great pleasure your letter of the 10th. of March. The mark, it affords of your kind attention, and the particular account it gives me of so many relations in Scotland are extremely gratifying to me. You no doubt have understood that my fathers affairs at a very early day went to wreck; so as to have rendered his situation during the greatest part of his life far from eligible. This state of things occasionned a separation between him and me, when I was very young, and threw me upon the bounty of my mothers relations, some of whom were then wealthy, though by vicissitudes to which human affairs are so liable, they have been since much reduced and broken up. Myself at about sixteen came to this Country. Having always had a strong propensity to literary pursuits, by a course of steady and laborious exertion, I was able, by the age of Ninteen to qualify myself for the degree of Batchelor of Arts in the College of New York, and to lay a foundation, by preparatory study, for the future profession of the law.

The American Revolution supervened. My principles led me to take part in it. At nineteen I entered into the American army as Captain of Artillery. Shortly after, I became by his invitation Aide De Camp to General Washington, in which station, I served till the commencement of that Campaign which ended with the seige of York, in Virginia, and the Capture of Cornwallis's Army. This Campaign I made at the head of a corps of light infantry, with which I was present at the seige of York and engaged in some interesting operations.

At the period of the peace with Great Britain, I found myself a member of Congress by appointment of the legislature of this State.

After the peace, I settled in the City of New York in the practice of the law; and was in a very lucrative course of practice, when the derangement of our public affairs, by the feebleness of the general confederation, drew me again reluctantly into public life. I became a member of the Convention which framed the present Constitution of the u states; and having taken part in this measure, I conceived myself to be under an obligation to lend my aid towards putting the machine in some regular motion. Hence I did not hesitate to accept the offer of President Washington to undertake the office of Secretary of the Treasury.

In that office, I met with many intrinsic difficulties, and many artificial ones proceeding from passions, not very worthy, common to human nature, and which act with peculiar force in republics. The object, however, was effected, of establishing public credit and introducing order into the finances.

Public Office in this Country has few attractions. The pecuniary emolument is so inconsiderable as to amount to a sacrifice to any man who can employ his time with advantage in any liberal profession. The opportunity of doing good, from the jealousy of power and the spirit of faction, is too small in any station to warrant a long continuance of private sacrifices. The enterprises of party had so far succeeded as materially to weaken the necessary influence and energy of the Executive Authority, and so far diminish the power of doing good in that department as greatly to take away the motives which a virtuous man might have for making sacrifices. The prospect was even bad for gratifying in future the love of Fame, if that passion was to be the spring of action.

The Union of these motives, with the reflections of prudence in relation to a growing family determined me as soon as my plan had attained a certain maturity to withdraw from Office. This I did by a resignation about two years since, when I resumed the profession of the law in the City of New York under every advantage I could desire.

It is a pleasing reflection to me that since the commencement of my connection with General Washington to the present time, I have possessed a flattering share of his confidence and friendship.

Having given you a brief sketch of my political career, I proceed to some further family details.

In the year 1780 I married the second daughter of General Schuyler, a Gentleman of one of the best families of this Country; of large fortune and no less personal and public consequence. It is impossible to be happier than I am in a wife and I have five Children, four sons and a daughter; the eldest a son somewhat passed fifteen, who all promise well, as far as their years permit and yield me much satisfaction. Though I have been too much in public life to be wealthy, my situation is extremely comfortable and leaves me nothing to wish but a continuance of health. With this blessing, the profits of my profession and other prospects authorise an expectation of such addition to my resources as will render the eve of life easy and agreeable; so far as may depend on this consideration.

It is now several months since I have heared from my father who continued at the Island of St Vincents. My anxiety at this silence would be greater than it is, were it not for the considerable interruption and precariousness of intercourse, which is produced by the War.

I have strongly pressed the old Gentleman to come to reside with me which would afford him every enjoyment of which his advanced age is capable. But he has declined it on the ground that the advice of his Physicians leads him to fear that, the change of Climate would be fatal to him. The next thing for me is, in proportion to my means to endeavour to increase his comforts where he is.

It will give me the greatest pleasure to receive your son Robert at my house in New York and still more to be of use to him; to which end my recommendation and interest will not be wanting, and, I hope, not unavailing. It is my intention to embrace the opening which your letter affords me to extend intercourse with my relations in your Country, which will be a new source of satisfaction to me.

TO AN UNIDENTIFIED FRIEND

When young, Hamilton wrote bantering letters to friends his own age. The one following, from camp at Morristown, was doubtless to Catherine Livingston, daughter of the Governor of New Jersey. The chaffing manner was never natural to Hamilton. The last paragraph, disavowing military ambition, is more in his vein. He had been aide to Washington only a couple of months at this time.

> Head Quarters. Morris Town
> May   1777

When I was almost out of patience and out of humour at your presumptous delay, in not showing yourself duly sensible of the honor done you, by me, your epistle opportunely came to hand, and has put all matters tolerably to rights.

As I thought it well enough written, and no discredit to you, I ventured to show it to a Gentleman of our family. He was silly enough to imagine, that I did this through vanity, and a desire to display my own importance, in having so fair and so sensible a correspondent; as he indulgently called you; but I hope you will not be so vain as to entertain, a single moment, the most distant imagination of the same kind. It would be paying yourself too high a compliment, and give room to suspect you are strongly infected with that extreme self-complacency, commonly attributed to your sex.

But as I have reason to believe this Gentleman has serious thoughts of becoming my rival, to give, at once, a mortal blow to all his hopes, I will recount what passed on this occasion. After attentive[ly] perusing your letter during which, the liveliest emotions [of] approbation were pictured in his face, 'Hamilton!' cries he, 'when you write to this divine girl again, it must be in [the] stile of adoration: none but a goddess, I am sure, could 'have penned so fine a letter!' As I know you have [an] invincible aversion to all flattery and extravagance, I [will] not be afraid, that a Quixot, capable of uttering him[self] perfectly in the language of knight-errantry, will ev[er be] able to supplant me in the good graces of a lady of yo[ur] sober understanding.

I am glad you are sensible of the oblig[ati]ons, you are under to me, for my benevolent and disinteres[ted] conduct, in making so currageous an effort, under all the imaginary terrors you intimate, without my tolerable prospect of compensation. I am very willing to continue my kindness, even though it meet with no better a return than in the last instance, provided you will stipulate on your part, that it shall meet with no worse. But to g[ive] a more perfect idea of what you owe me for this condes[cending] generosity, let me inform you, that I exercise it at th[e risk] of being anathematized by grave censors, for dedicating so much of my time, to so trifling and insignificant a toy as a woman; and, on the other hand, of being run through the body by saucy inamorato's, who will envy me the prodigious favour, forsooth, of your correspondence. So that between the morose apathy of some and the envious Sensibility of others, I shall probably be in a fine way. But ALL FOR LOVE is my motto. You may make what comments you please. Now for politics——

'Tis believed by our military Connoisseurs, that the enemy are preparing to quit the Jerseys, and make some expedition by water. Many suppose up the North River. But my opinion is, that, if they abandon the Jerseys, they will content themselves with enjoying quiet quarters on Staten Island, 'till re-inforced. Perhaps, however, the appearances, which give rise to an opinion of an evacuation of the Jerseys, are only preparatory to an attack upon us. They would admit such an interpretation, if an attempt of the kind were not too hazardous to be consistent with prudence. Should they leave this State, your return home would be the more safe and agreeable; but you need not be precipitate.

Your sentiments respecting war are perfec[tly] just. I do not wonder at your antipathy to it. Every finer feeling of a delicate mind revolts from the idea of sheding human blood and multiplying the common evils o[f] life by the artificial methods incident to that state. Were it not for the evident necessity and in defence of all that is valuable in society, I could never be reconciled to a mili-[tary] character; and shall rejoice when the restoration of pe[ace] on the basis of freedom and independence shall put it [in] my power to renounce it. That my fugitive friend [will] soon be restored to those peaceful and secure abodes, she [hopes] for, is not more her own wish, than that of

Alexr. Hamilton

TO ELIZABETH SCHUYLER

Numerous writers, from a quick look at circumstantial evidence, have declared that Hamilton married Elizabeth, the daughter of General Philip Schuyler, for money and social position rather than for love. The following letter to her, late in their engagement, is a refutation of that idea. It is now first printed through the courtesy of the owner, Mrs. John C. Hamilton of Elmsford, New York.

Impatiently My Dearest have I been expecting the return of your father to bring me a letter from my charmer with the answers you have been good enough to promise me to the little questions asked in mine by him. I long to see the workings of my Betseys heart, and I promise my self I shall have ample gratification to my fondness in the sweet familiarly of her pen. She will there I hope paint me her feelings without reserve—even in those tender moments of pillowed retirement, when her soul abstracted from every other object, delivers it self up to love and to me, yet with all that delicacy which suits the purity of her mind and which is so conspicuous in whatever she does.

It is now a week my Betsey since I have heard from you. In that time I have written you twice. I think it will be adviseable in future to number our letters, for I have reason to suspect they do not all meet with fair play. This is number one.

Meade just comes in and interrupts me by sending his love to you. He tells you he has written a long letter to his widow asking her opinion of the propriety of quitting the service; and that if she does not disapprove it, he will certainly take his final leave after the campaign. You see what a fine opportunity she has to be enrolled in the catalogue of heroines, and I dare say she will set you an example of fortitude and patriotism. I know too you have so much of the Portia in you, that you will not be out done in this line by any of your sex, and that if you saw me inclined to quit the service of your country, you would dissuade me from it. I have promised you, you recollect, to conform to your wishes, and I persist in this intention.

It remains with you to show whether you are a *Roman* or an *American wife.*

Though I am not sanguine in expecting it, I am not without hopes this Winter will produce a peace and then you must submit to the mortification of enjoying more domestic happiness and less fame. This I know you will not like but we cannot always have things as we wish.

The affairs of England are in so bad a plight that if no fortunate events attend her this campaign, it would seem impossible for her to proceed in the war. But she is an obstinate old dame, and seems determined to ruin her whole family, rather than to let Miss America go on flirting it with her new lovers, with whom, as giddy young girls often do, she eloped in contempt of her mothers authority. I know you will be ready to justify her conduct and to tell me the ill treatment she received was enough to make any girl of spirit act in the same manner. But I will one day cure you of these refractory notions about the right of resistance, (of which I foresee you will be apt to make a very dangerous application), and teach you the great advantage and absolute necessity of implicit obedience.

But now we are talking of times to come, tell me my pretty damsel have you made up your mind upon the subject of housekeeping? Do you soberly relish the pleasure of being a poor mans wife? Have you learned to think a home spun preferable to a brocade and the rumbling of a waggon wheel to the musical rattling of a coach and six? Will you be able to see with perfect composure your old acquaintances flaunting it in gay life—tripping it along in elegance and splendor—while you hold an humble station and have no other enjoyments than the sober comforts of a good wife? Can you in short be an Aquileia and chearfully plant turnips with me, if fortune should so order it? If you cannot my Dear we are playing a comedy of all in the wrong, and you should correct the mistake before we begin to act the tragedy of the unhappy couple.

I propose you a set of new questions my lovely girl; but though they are asked with an air of levity, they merit a very serious consideration, for on their being resolved in the affirmative stripped of all the colorings of a fond imagination our happiness may absolutely depend. I have not concealed my circumstances from my Betsey— they are far from splendid—they may possibly even be worse than I expect, for every day brings me fresh proof of the knavery of those to whom my little affairs are entrusted. They have already filed down what was in their hands more than one half, and I am told they go on diminishing it, 'till I *fear* they will reduce it below my *former fears*. An indifference to property enters into my character too much, and what affects me now as my Betsey is concerned in it, I should have laughed at or not thought of at all a year ago. But I have thoroughly examined my own heart. Beloved by you, I can be happy in any situation, and can struggle with every embarrassment of fortune with patience and firmness. I cannot however forbear entreating you to realize our union on the dark side and satisfy, without deceiving yourself, how far your affection for me can make you happy in a privation of those elegancies to which you have been accustomed. If fortune should smile upon us, it will do us no harm to have been prepared for adversity; if she frowns upon us, by being prepared, we shall encounter it without the chagrin of disappointment. Your future rank in life is a perfect lottery—you may move in exalted, you may move in a very humble sphere—the last is most probable; examine well your heart. And in doing it dont figure to yourself a cottage in romance with the spontaneous bounties of nature courting you to enjoyment. Dont imagine yourself a shepherdess—your hair embroidered with flowers a crook in your hand tending your flock under a shady tree, by the side of a cool fountain—your faithful shepherd sitting near and entertaining you with gentle tales of love. These are pretty dreams and very apt to enter into the heads of lovers when they think of a connection without the advantages of fortune. But they must not be indulged. You must apply your situation to real life, and think how you should feel in scenes of which you may find examples every day. So far My Dear Betsey as the tenderest affection can compensate for other inconveniences in making your estimate, you cannot give too large a credit for this article. My heart overflows with every thing for you that admiration, esteem and love can inspire—*I would this moment give the world to be near you only to kiss your sweet hand.* Believe what I say to be truth and imagine what are my feelings when I say it. Let it awake your sympathy and let our hearts melt in a prayer to be soon united, never more to be separated

Adieu loveliest of your sex

AH

Instead of inclosing your letter to your father I inclose his to you because I do not know whether he may not be on his way here. If he is at home he will tell you the military news. If he has set out for camp, you may open and read my letters to him. The one from Mr. Mathews you will return by the first opportunity

received the beginning of Sepr.

TO ELIZABETH SCHUYLER

Hamilton, with Generals Washington, Lafayette, Knox, and others, returning to the Hudson from Hartford where they had met the French, witnessed the sequel of Benedict Arnold's treason. Hamilton narrated the ugly circumstances in a full letter to John Laurens, which was widely published. The shorter description below betrays as much his tenderness for his fiancée as for Peggy Arnold. Some recent students are satisfied that the traitor's wife was privy to his plot, and feigned her distress which so moved Hamilton.

September 25, 1780

Arnold hearing of the plot being detected immediately fled to the enemy. I went in pursuit of him, but was much too late and could hardly regret the disappointment when on my return, I saw an amiable woman, frantic with distress for the loss of a husband she tenderly loved—a traitor to his country and to his fame—a disgrace to his connections: it was the most affecting scene I ever was witness to. She for a considerable time, entirely lost herself. The General went up to see her, and she upbraided him with being in a plot to murder her child. One moment she raved another she melted into tears. Sometimes she pressed her infant to her bosom, and lamented its fate, occasioned by the imprudence of its father in a manner that would have pierced insensibility itself. All the sweetness of beauty, all the loveliness of innocence, all the tenderness of a wife and all the fondness of a mother showed themselves in her appearance and conduct. We have every reason to believe that she was entirely unacquainted with the plan; and that the first knowledge of it was when Arnold went to tell her he must banish himself from his country and from her forever. She instantly fell into a convulsion, and he left her in that situation.

This morning she is more composed. I paid her a visit and endeavored to soothe her by every method in my power, though you may imagine she is not easily to be consoled. Added to her other distresses she is very apprehensive the resentment of her country will fall upon her (who is only unfortunate) for the guilt of her husband.

I have tried to persuade her that her fears are un-founded, but she will not be convinced. She received us in bed with every circumstance that interests our sympathy, and her sufferings were so eloquent that I wished myself her brother to have a right to become her defender. As it is, I have entreated her to enable me to give her proofs of my friendship. Could I forgive Arnold for sacrificing his honor, reputation, and duty, I could not forgive him for acting a part that must have forfeited the esteem of so fine a woman. At present she almost forgets his crime in his misfortunes; and her horror at the guilt of the traitor is lost in her love of the man. But a virtuous mind cannot long esteem a base one; and time will make her despise if it cannot make her hate.

TO PHILIP SCHUYLER

The following explanation to his father-in-law is the main source of our knowledge of Hamilton's single personal difference with Washington. He had served at headquarters four years, much of that time "as the *principal and most confidential aid* of the Commander in Chief."

The tiff happened when both were under extraordinary strain. Though precocious, Hamilton was not mature enough to respond to Washington's overture for immediate erasure of hasty words. However, the break was brief, for Hamilton was soon back in camp, receiving from the forgiving Washington his long-sought field command (for the Virginia campaign). After the war their cooperation was the most fruitful ever.

Headquarters, New Windsor, February 18, 1781.

My Dear Sir:

Since I had the pleasure of writing you last, an unexpected change has taken place in my situation. I am no longer a member of the General's family. This information will surprise you, and the manner of the change will surprise you more. Two days ago, the General and I passed each other on the stairs. He told me he wanted to speak to me. I answered that I would wait upon him immediately. I went below, and delivered Mr. Tilghman a letter to be sent to the commissary, containing an order of a pressing and interesting nature.

Returning to the General, I was stopped on the way by the Marquis de La Fayette, and we conversed together about a minute on a matter of business. He can testify how impatient I was to get back, and that I left him in a manner which, but for our intimacy, would have been more than abrupt. Instead of finding the General, as is usual, in his room, I met him at the head of the stairs, where, accosting me in an angry tone, "Colonel Hamilton," said he, "you have kept me waiting at the head of the stairs these ten minutes. I must tell you, sir, you treat me with disrespect." I replied, without petulancy, but with decision: "I am not conscious of it, sir; but since you have thought it necessary to tell me so, we part." "Very well, sir," said he, "if it be your choice," or something to this effect, and we separated. I sincerely believe my absence, which gave so much umbrage, did not last two minutes.

In less than an hour after, Tilghman came to me in the General's name, assuring me of his great confidence in my abilities, integrity, usefulness, etc., and of his desire, in a candid conversation, to heal a difference which could not have happened but in a moment of passion. I requested Mr. Tilghman to tell him—1st. That I had taken my resolution in a manner not to be revoked. 2d. That, as a conversation could serve no other purpose than to produce explanations, mutually disagreeable, though I certainly would not refuse an interview if he desired it, yet I would be happy if he would permit me to decline it. 3d. That, though determined to leave the family, the same principles which had kept me so long in it would continue to direct my conduct towards him when out of it. 4th. That, however, I did not wish to distress him, or the public business, by quitting him before he could derive other assistance by the return of some of the gentlemen who were absent. 5th. And that, in the mean time, it depended on him to let our behavior to each other be the same as if nothing had happened. He consented to decline the conversation, and thanked me for my offer of continuing my aid in the manner I had mentioned. Thus we stand. I wait Mr. Humphrey's return from the eastward, and may be induced to wait the return of Mr. Harrison from Virginia.

I have given you so particular a detail of our difference from the desire I have to justify myself in your opinion. Perhaps you may think I was precipitate in rejecting the overture made by the General to an accommodation. I assure you, my dear sir, it was not the effect of resentment; it was the deliberate result of maxims I had long formed for the government of my own conduct.

TO ELIZABETH HAMILTON

The four following letters (one a fragment) reveal his solicitude for his wife during the Virginia campaign that ended in the surrender of Cornwallis. Five months pregnant, she was at first prostrated by news of Hamilton's dangerous errand. The first letter was probably from Washington's camp at Dobbs Ferry, New York. Three days after the last, Cornwallis's capitulation was signed in the redoubt which Hamilton's force had captured. Immediately Hamilton wore out his horses in his anxiety to rejoin Elizabeth at Albany.

August, 1781.

In my last letter I informed you that there was a greater prospect of activity now, than there had been heretofore. I did this to prepare your mind for an event which, I am sure, will give you pain. I begged your father, at the same time, to intimate to you, by degrees, the probability of its taking place. I used this method to prevent a surprise, which might be too severe to you. A part of the army, my dear girl, is going to Virginia, and I must, of necessity, be separated at a much greater distance from my beloved wife. I cannot announce the fatal necessity, without feeling every thing that a fond husband can feel. I am unhappy; I am unhappy beyond expression. I am unhappy, because I am to be so remote from you; because I am to hear from you less frequently than I am accustomed to do. I am miserable, because I know you will be so; I am wretched at the idea of flying so far from you, without a single hour's interview, to tell you all my pains and all my love. But I cannot ask permission to visit you. It might be thought improper to leave my corps at such a time and upon such an occasion. I must go without seeing you—I must go without embracing you;—alas! I must go. But let no idea, other than of the distance we shall be asunder, disquiet you. Though I said the prospects of activity will be greater, I said it to give your expectations a different turn, and prepare you for something disagreeable. It is ten to one that our views will be disappointed, by Cornwallis retiring to South Carolina by land. At all events, our operations will be over by the latter end of October, and I will fly to my home. Don't mention I am going to Virginia.

Head of Elk, Sept. 6, 1781.

Yesterday, my lovely wife, I wrote to you, inclosing you a letter in one to your father, to the care of Mr. Morris. To-morrow the post sets out, and to-morrow we embark for Yorktown. I cannot refuse myself the pleasure of writing you a few lines. Constantly uppermost in my thoughts and affections, I am happy only when my moments are devoted to some office that respects you. I would give the world to be able to tell you all I feel and all I wish, but consult your own heart and you will know mine. What a world will soon be between us! To support the idea, all my fortitude is insufficient. What must be the case with you, who have the most female of female hearts? I sink at the perspective of your distress, and I look to heaven to be your guardian and supporter. Circumstances that have just come to my knowledge assure me that our operations will be expeditious, as well as our success certain. Early in November, as I promised you, we shall certainly meet. Cheer yourself with this idea, and with the assurance of never more being separated. Every day confirms me in the intention of renouncing public life and devoting myself wholly to you. Let others waste their time and their tranquillity in a vain pursuit of power and glory; be it my object to be happy in a quiet retreat with my better angel.

September, 1781.

How chequered is human life! How precarious is happiness! How easily do we often part with it for a shadow! These are the reflections that frequently intrude themselves upon me with a painful application. I am going to do my duty. Our operations will be so conducted as to economize the lives of men. Exert your fortitude and rely upon heaven.

Yorktown, Oct. 16, 1781.

Two nights ago, my Eliza, my duty and my honor obliged me to take a step in which your happiness was too much risked. I commanded an attack upon one of the enemy's redoubts; we carried it in an instant, and with little loss. You will see the particulars in the Philadelphia papers. There will be, certainly, nothing more of this kind; all the rest will be by approach; and if there should be another occasion, it will not fall to my turn to execute it.

TO GENERAL HENRY KNOX

The youthful Captain Charles Asgill, a British prisoner in American hands, was selected by lot and ordered executed in reprisal for the hanging by the enemy of the American Captain Joshua Huddy. General

Washington and the other American authorities held Huddy to be innocent. Sir Henry Clinton (and later Sir Guy Carleton) refused to surrender Captain Lippincott, who was responsible for Huddy's death.
Washington seemed adamant for retaliation. Hamilton's compassionate
and wise remonstrance was matched by his merciful attitude on other
occasions, notably his plea that the doomed André might be shot, not
hanged. After agonizing months Asgill was released, but not until his
mother entreated the king and queen of France to intervene.

Dr General

We are told here that there is a British officer coming on from
Cornwallis's army to be executed by way of retaliation for the murder of Capt Huddy. As this appears to me clearly to be an ill-timed
proceeding, and if persisted in will be derogatory to the national
character I cannot forbear communicating to you my ideas upon
the subject. A sacrifice of this sort is entirely repugnant to the
genius of the age we live in and is without example in modern history nor can it fail to be considered in Europe as wanton and unnecessary. It appears that the enemy (from necessity I grant but the
operation is the same) have changed their system and adopted a
more humane one; and therefore the only justifying motive of retaliation, the preventing a repetition of cruelty, ceases. But if this were
not the case, so solemn and deliberate a sacrifice of the innocent for
the guilty must be condemned on the present received notions of
humanity, and encourage an opinion that we are in a certain degree
in a state of barbarism. Our affairs are now in a prosperous train,
and so vigorous, I would rather say so violent a measure would want
the plea of necessity. It would argue meanness in us that at this late
stage of the war, in the midst of success, we should suddenly depart
from that temper with which we have all along borne with as great
and more frequent provocation. The death of André could not have
been dispensed with; but it must still be viewed at a distance as an
act of *rigid justice*. If we wreak our resentment on an innocent person, it will be suspected that we are too fond of executions. I am
persuaded it will have an influence peculiarly unfavourable to the
General's character.

If it is seriously believed that in this advanced stage of affairs retaliation is necessary let another mode be chosen. Let under actors be employed, and let the authority by which it is done be wrapt in obscurity and doubt. Let us endeavour to make it fall upon those who have had a direct or indirect share in the guilt. Let not the Commander-in-Chief considered as the first and most respectable character among us come forward in person and be the avowed author of an act at which every humane feeling revolts. Let us at least have as much address as the enemy, and, if we must have victims appoint some obscure agents to perform the ceremony, and bear the odium which must always attend even justice itself when directed by extreme severity.

For my own part, my Dear Sir I think a business of this complexion entirely out of season. The time for it, if there ever was one, is past.

But it is said that the Commander-in-Chief has pledged himself for it and cannot recede. Inconsistency in this case would be better than consistency. But pretext may be found and will be readily admitted in favor of humanity. Carleton will in all probability do something like apology and concession. He will give assurance, of preventing every thing of the kind in future. Let the General appear to be satisfied with these assurances. The steps Carleton is said to have taken to suppress the refugee incursions will give the better color to lenity.

I address myself to you upon this occasion because I know your liberality and your influence with the General. If you are of my opinion I am sure you will employ it—if it should not be too late. I would not think a letter necessary, but I know how apt men are to be actuated by the circumstances which immediately surround them, and to be led into an approbation of measures which in another situation they would disapprove. Mrs. Hamilton joins me in compliments to Mrs. Knox; Believe me to be very truly & Affectly
Dr Sir

Yr Obed Svt

A. Hamilton.

Albany June 7 '82

TO JOHN LAURENS

The similar verve, gallantry, and public spirit of John Laurens and Hamilton drew them into intimacy on Washington's staff, in plans for Laurens's successful mission for succor from France, and in the capture of a British redoubt at Yorktown. The young South Carolinian was the son of Henry Laurens, who had been president of the Continental Congress. He probably never received Hamilton's comradely plea, for he fell before an enemy ambush in his native state a fortnight later. The news brought Hamilton "the deepest affliction."

I received with great pleasure, My Dear Laurens, the letter which you wrote me in —— last. Your wishes in one respect are gratified, this state has pretty unanimously delegated me to Congress. My time of service commences in November. It is not probable it will result in what you mention. I hope it is too late. We have great reason to flatter ourselves peace on our own terms is upon the carpet. The making it is in good hands. It is said your father is exchanged for Cornwallis and gone to Paris to meet the other commissioners and that Granville on the part of England has made a second trip there, in the last instance vested with Plenipotentiary powers.

I fear there may be obstacles but I hope they may be surmounted.

Peace made, my Dear friend, a new scene opens. The object then will be to make our independence a blessing. To do this we must secure our *union* on solid foundations; an herculean task and to effect which, mountains of prejudice must be levelled! It requires all the virtue and all the abilities of the Country. Quit your sword my friend, put on the *toga*, come to Congress. We know each other's sentiments our views are the same: we have fought side by side to make America free, let us hand in hand struggle to make her happy. Remember me to General Greene with all the warmth of sincere attachment. Yours forever.

A Hamilton

Albany   Augt. 15. 1782

TO GENERAL NATHANAEL GREENE

Dr General

It is an age since I have either written to you or received a line from you; yet I persuade myself you have not been the less convinced of my affectionate attachment and warm participation in all those events which have given you that place in your countrys esteem and approbation which I have known you to deserve while your enemies and rivals were most active in sullying your reputation.

You will perhaps learn before this reaches you that I have been appointed a member of Congress. I expect to go to Philadelphia in the ensuing month, where I shall be happy to correspond with you with our ancient confidence and I shall entreat you not to confine your observations to military subjects but to take in the whole scope of national concerns. I am sure your ideas will be useful to me and to the public.

I feel the deepest affliction at the news we have just received of the loss of our dear and inestimable friend Laurens. His career of virtue is at an end. How strangely are human affairs conducted, that so many excellent qualities could not ensure a more happy fate? The world will feel the loss of a man who has left few like him behind, and America of a citizen whose heart realized that patriotism of which others only talk. I feel the loss of a friend I truly and most tenderly loved, and one of a very small number.

I take the liberty to inclose you a letter to Mr. Kane Executor to the estate of Mr. Lavine a half Brother of mine who died some time since in South Carolina. Capt Roberts, if you should not be acquainted with him, can inform you who he is. I shall be much obliged to you to have my letter carefully forwarded.

Mrs Hamilton sends her particular compliments to Mrs Greene & yourself; to the former please to join mine

I am Dr. Sir

truly Yr. friend & serv

A Hamilton

Albany October 12. 1782
General Greene

TO COLONEL RICHARD K. MEADE

"Friend Dick," as General Washington called him with fatherly affection, was Hamilton's fellow-aide and abiding friend, though their paths diverged. Meade became a planter in his native Virginia, and the father of a celebrated bishop. Hamilton's first child, here described, was Philip, the most talented of eight brothers and sisters. He graduated from Columbia College, but his promising career was cut short at twenty by a duel at Weehawken, New Jersey, where his father was to fall two years later.

Albany, August 27, 1782.

I thank you, my dear Meade, for your letter of the first of this month, which you will perceive has travelled much faster than has been usual with our letters. Our correspondence hitherto has been unfortunate; nor, in fact, can either of us compliment himself on his punctuality, but you were right in concluding that, however indolence or accident may interrupt our intercourse, nothing will interrupt our friendship. Mine for you is built on a solid basis of a full conviction that you deserve it, and that it is reciprocal; and it is the more firmly fixed because you have few competitors. Experience is a continual comment on the worthlessness of the human race; and the few exceptions we find have the greater right to be valued in proportion as they are rare. I know few men estimable, few amiable; and when I meet with one of the last description, it is not in my power to withhold my affection.

You reproach me with not having said enough about our little stranger. When I wrote last I was not sufficiently acquainted with him to give you his character. I may now assure you that your daughter, when she sees him, will not consult you about the choice, or will only do it in respect to the rules of decorum. He is truly a very fine young gentleman, the most agreeable in his conversation and his intelligence and sweetness of temper. You are not to imagine, by my beginning with his mental qualifications, that he is defective in personal. It is agreed on all hands that he is handsome; his features are good, his eye is not only sprightly and expressive, but full of benignity. His attitude in sitting, is, by connoisseurs, esteemed graceful, and he has a method of waving his hand that announces the future orator. He stands, however, rather awkwardly, and as his legs have not all the delicate slimness of his father's, it is feared he may never excel as much in dancing, which is probably the only accomplishment in which he will not be a model. If he has any fault in manners, he laughs too much. He has now passed his seventh month. I am glad to find your prospect of being settled approaches. I am sure you will realize all the happiness you promise yourself with your amiable partner. I wish fortune had not cast our lots at such a distance. Mrs. Meade, you, Betsey, and myself would make a most affectionate and most happy *partie quarre*.

As to myself, I shall sit down in New York when it opens; and this period, we are told, approaches. No man looks forward to a peace with more pleasure than I do; though no man would sacrifice less to it than myself if I were not convinced that the people sigh for peace.

I have been studying the law for some months, and have lately been licensed as an attorney. I wish to prepare myself by October for examination as a counsellor; but some public avocation may possibly prevent me.

I had almost forgotten to tell you that I have been pretty unanimously elected, by the Legislature of this State, a member of Congress, to begin to serve in November. I do not hope to reform the State, although I shall endeavor to do all the good I can.

Suffer Betsey and me to present our love to Mrs. Meade. She has a sisterly affection for you. My respects, if you please, to Mr. and Mrs. Fitzhugh. God bless you.

TO THE MARQUIS DE LAFAYETTE

Hamilton sometimes suffered reactions from his intense efforts in the public behalf, when he would express indifference or even disgust. But these moods of disillusionment never lasted long.

Since we parted My Dear Marquis at York Town I have received three letters from you one written on your way to Boston, two from France. I acknowlege that I have written to you only once, but the reason has been that I have been taught dayly to expect your return. This I should not have done from my own calculations; for I saw no prospect but of an inactive campaign, and you had much better be intriguing for your hobby horse at Paris than loitering away your time here. Yet they seemed to be convinced at Head Quarters that you were certainly coming out; and [as] by your letters it appears to have been your own expectation, I imagine you have relinquished it by this time.

I have been employed for the last ten months in rocking the cradle and studying the art of fleecing my neighbours. I am now a grave Counsellor at law, and shall soon be a grave member of Congress. The Legislature at their last session took it into their heads to name me pretty unanimously one of their delegates. I am going to throw away a few months more in public life and then I retire a simple citizen and good paterfamilias. I set out for Philadelphia in a few days. You see the disposition I am in. You are condemned to run the race of ambition all your life. I am already tired of the career and dare to leave it.

But you would not give a pin for my letter unless politics or war made a part of it. You tell me they are employed in building a *peace*. [And other] accounts say it is nearly finished; I hope the work may meet with no interruptions. It is necessary for America; especially if your army is taken from us as we are told will soon be the case. That was an essential *point d'appui*. Though money was the *primum mobile* of our finances, which must now lose the little activity lately given them. Our trade is prodigiously cramped. These states are in no humour for continuing exertions: if the war lasts, it must be carried on by external succours. I make no apology for the inertness of this country. I detest it, but since it exists I am sorry to see other resources diminish.

Your Ministers ought to know best what they are doing; but if the war goes on and the removal of the army does not prove an unwise measure I renounce all future pretentions to judgment. I think however the circumstances of the enemy oblige them to peace.

We have been hoping that they would abandon their posts in these states; it no doubt was once in contemplation, but latter appearances are rather ambiguous. I begin to suspect that if Peace is not made New York & Charles Town, the former at least will still be held.

There is no probability that I shall be one of the Commissioners for peace. It is a thing I do not desire myself and which I imagine other people will not desire.

Our army is now in excellent order but small.

The temper we are in respecting the alliance you will see from public acts. There never was a time of greater unanimity on that point.

I wish I durst enter into a greater detour with you but our cypher is not fit for it and I fear to trust it in another shape.

Is there anything you wish on this side the water? You know the warmth & sincerity of my attachment. Command me.

I have not been so happy as to see Mr. De Segur. The title of your friend would have been a title to every thing in my power to manifest.

Adieu

General & Mrs. Schuyler & Mrs. Hamilton all join warmly in the most affectionate remembrances to you. As to myself I am in truth yours pour *la vie*

AH

I wrote a long letter to the Viscount De Noailles whom I also love. Has he received it? Is the worthy Gouvion well? Has he succeeded? How is it with our friend Gimat? How is it with General Du Portail; all those men are men of merit & interest my best wishes.

Poor Laurens; he has fallen a sacrifice to his ardor in a trifling skirmish in South Carolina. You know how truly I loved him and will judge how much I regret him.

I will write you again soon after my arrival at Philadelphia.

Albany November 3d. 1782

TO JOHN JAY

The principal achievement of Hamilton was in helping America to reap the fruits of independence. Immediately the peace treaty was signed— indeed, before that—he was looking forward to reforms in government.

Philadelphia, July 25, 1783

Dear Sir:

Though I have not performed my promise of writing to you which I made you when you left this country, yet I have not the less interested myself in your welfare and success. I have been witness with pleasure to every event which has had a tendency to advance you in the esteem of your country, and I may assure you with sincerity that it is as high as you could possibly wish. All have united in the warmest approbation of your conduct. I cannot forbear telling you this, because my situation has given me access to the truth, and I gratify my friendship for you in communicating what cannot fail to gratify your sensibility.

The peace, which exceeds in the goodness of its terms the expectations of the most sanguine, does the highest honor to those who made it. It is the more agreeable, as the time was come when thinking men began to be seriously alarmed at the internal embarrassments and exhausted state of this country. The New England people talk of making you an annual fish-offering, as an acknowledgment of your exertions for the participation of the fisheries. We have now happily concluded the great work of independence, but much remains to be done to reap the fruits of it. Our prospects are not flattering. Every day proves the inefficiency of the present Confederation; yet the common danger being removed, we are receding instead of advancing in the disposition to amend its defects. The road to popularity in each State is to inspire jealousies of the power of Congress, though nothing can be more apparent than that they have no power; and that for the want of it, the resources of the country during the war could not be drawn out, and we at this moment experience all the mischiefs of a bankrupt and ruined credit.

It is to be hoped that when prejudice and folly have run themselves out of breath, we may return to reason and correct our errors. After having served in the field during the war, I have been making a short apprenticeship in Congress, but the evacuation of New York approaching, I am preparing to take leave of public life, to enter into the practice of the law. Your country will continue to demand your services abroad. I beg you to present me most respectfully to Mrs. Jay, and to be assured, etc.

TO JAMES HAMILTON, JR.

James Hamilton was Alexander's full brother, two years older than himself. He was apprenticed to a carpenter on the island of St. Croix, and we catch only uncertain glimpses of him thereafter. Their father, James Hamilton, Sr., had left the family twenty years before the following solicitous inquiry was penned. Alexander later forwarded money to his father on several occasions, but did not see him before his death on St. Vincent at an advanced age.

My dear Brother: New York, June 22, 1785

I have received your letter of the 31st of May last, which, and one other, are the only letters I have received from you in many years. I am a little surprised you did not receive one which I wrote to you about six months ago. The situation you describe yourself to be in gives me much pain, and nothing will make me happier than, as far as may be in my power, to contribute to your relief. I will cheerfully pay your draft upon me for fifty pounds sterling, whenever it shall appear. I wish it was in my power to desire you to enlarge the sum; but though my future prospects are of the most flattering kind my present engagements would render it inconvenient to me to advance you a larger sum. My affection for you, however, will not permit me to be inattentive to your welfare, and I hope time will prove to you that I feel all the sentiment of a brother. Let me only request of you to exert your industry for a year or two more where you are, and at the end of that time I promise myself to be able to invite you to a more comfortable settlement in this country. Allow me only to give you one caution, which is to avoid if possible getting in debt. Are you *married* or *single?* If the *latter*, it is my wish for many reasons it may be agreeable to you to continue in that state.

But what has become of our dear father? It is an age since I have heard from him or of him, though I have written him several letters. Perhaps, alas! he is no more, and I shall not have the pleasing opportunity of contributing to render the close of his life more happy than the progress of it. My heart bleeds at the recollection of his misfortunes and embarrasments. Sometimes I flatter myself his brothers have extended their support to him, and that he now enjoys tranquillity and ease. At other times I fear he is suffering in indigence. I entreat you, if you can, to relieve me from my doubts, and let me know how or where he is, if alive, if dead, how and where he died. Should he be alive inform him of my inquiries, beg him to write to me, and tell him how ready I shall be to devote myself and all I have to his accommodation and happiness.

I do not advise your coming to this country at present, for the war has also put things out of order here, and people in your business find a subsistence difficult enough. My object will be, by-and-by, to get you settled on a farm.

Believe me always your affectionate friend and brother,

Alex. Hamilton

TO GENERAL GEORGE WASHINGTON

While delegates were constructing the Constitution in Philadelphia, Hamilton took leave for a while in New York. There, in newspaper pieces, he assailed Governor George Clinton for opposing the Convention. Out of this controversy grew the charge against Hamilton for which he sought, and at once obtained, Washington's denial.

D Sir/

You probably saw some time since some animadversions on certain expressions of Governor Clinton respecting the Convention. You may have seen a piece signed a Republican, attempting to bring the fact into question and endeavouring to controvert the conclusions drawn from it, if true. My answer you will find in the inclosed. I trouble you with it merely from that anxiety which is natural to every man to have his veracity at least stand in a fair light. The matter seems to be given up by the Governor and the fact with the inferences from it stand against him in full force, and operate as they ought to do.

It is however, of some importance to the party to diminish whatever credit or influence I may possess; and to effect this they stick at nothing. Among many contemptible artifices practiced by them, they have had recourse to an insinuation that I *palmed* myself upon you and that you *dismissed* me from your family. This I confess hurts my feelings, and if it obtains credit, will require a contradiction.

You Sir will undoubtedly recollect the manner in which I came into your family and went out of it; and know how destitute of foundation such insinuations are. My confidence in your justice will not permit me to doubt your readiness to put the matter in its true light in your answer to this letter. It cannot be my wish to give any complexion to the affair which might excite the least scruple in you; but I confess it would mortify me to be under the imputation either of having obtruded myself into the family of a General or of having been turned out of it.

The New Constitution is as popular in this City as it is possible for any thing to be, and the prospect thus far is favourable to it throughout the state. But there is no saying what turn things may take when the full flood of official influence is let loose against it. This is to be expected, for though the Governor has not publicly declared himself his particular connections and confidential friends are loud against it.

I remain with perfect esteem

Yr. Excellency's obed Ser

A Hamilton

Mrs Hamilton joins in respectful compliments to Mrs. Washington

General Washington

SPEECH IN THE
POUGHKEEPSIE CONVENTION

The following passage is from the close of an earnest speech, June 28, 1788, in the Poughkeepsie convention. Hamilton and his friends, striving for ratification of the Constitution by New York, embarrassed Governor George Clinton, their chief opponent. They showed that during the war he himself had deplored the financial weakness of the Confederation, and the extra burden placed on New York by states which did not respond to appeals of Congress. Hamilton did not mean to discredit Clinton, but to stigmatize the old, bad system. He tried to remove Clinton's personal resentment by a free apology if he had offended. At the same time he disavowed any selfish or class motive in espousing the Constitution.

I shall conclude with a few remarks by way of an apology. I am apprehensive, sir, that, in the warmth of my feelings, I may have uttered expressions which were too vehement. If such has been my language it was from the habit of using strong phrases to express my ideas; and, above all, from the interesting nature of the subject. I have ever condemned those cold, unfeeling hearts, which no object can animate. I condemn those indifferent mortals, who either never form opinions, or never make them known. I confess, sir, that on no subject has my breast been filled with stronger emotions or more anxious concern. If any thing has escaped me, which may be construed into a personal reflection, I beg the gentlemen, once for all, to be assured that I have no design to wound the feelings of any one who is opposed to me. While I am making these observations, I cannot but take notice of some expressions which have fallen in the course of the debate. It has been said that ingenious men may say ingenious things, and that those who are interested in raising the few upon the ruins of the many, may give to every cause an appearance of justice. I know not whether these insinuations allude to the characters of any who are present, or to any of the reasonings of the House. I presume that the gentlemen would not ungenerously impute such motives to those who differ from themselves. I declare I know not any set of men who are to derive peculiar advantages from this Constitution. Were any permanent honors or emoluments to be secured to the families of those who have been active in this cause, there might be some grounds for suspicion. But what reasonable man, for the precarious enjoyment of rank and power, would establish a system which would reduce his nearest friends and his posterity to slavery and ruin? If the gentlemen reckon me amongst the obnoxious few, if they imagine that I contemplate with ambitious eye the immediate honors of the government, yet let them consider that I have my friends, my family, my children, to whom ties of nature and of habit have attached me. If, to-day, I am among the favored few, my children, to-morrow, may be among the oppressed; these dear pledges of my patriotism may, at a future day, be suffering the severe distresses to which my ambition has reduced them. The changes in the human condition are uncertain and frequent; many, on whom fortune has bestowed her favors, may trace their family to a more unprosperous station; and many, who are now in obscurity, may look back upon the affluence and exalted rank of their ancestors. But I will no longer trespass on your indulgence. I have troubled the committee with these observations, to show that it cannot be the wish of any reasonable man to establish a government unfriendly to the liberties of the people. Gentlemen ought not, then, to presume that the advocates of this Constitution are influenced by ambitious views. The suspicion, sir, is unjust; the charge is uncharitable.

TO GENERAL GEORGE WASHINGTON

The following letter opens with a trifle, then refers to Hamilton's efforts to launch the new government prosperously. The papers of Publius are best known as *The Federalist*. At other times, too, Hamilton begged Washington to forfeit his desire for retirement, and become the first President.

Sir

Capt Cochran of the British navy has requested my aid in recovering a family watch worn by his brother, who fell at York Town (and now in the possession of —— ——). In compliance with his request I have written the letter herewith (to —— ——) which I take the liberty to convey through you, in hope that if you see no impropriety in it, you would add your influence to the endeavour to gratify Capt Cochran. It is one of those things in which the affections are apt to be interested, beyond the value of the object; and in which one naturally feels an inclination to oblige.

I have delivered to Mr. Madison to be forwarded to you a sett of the papers under the signature of Publius, neatly enough bound, to be honored with a place in your library. I presume you have understood that the writers of those Papers are chiefly Mr. Madison & myself with some aid from Mr. Jay.

I take it for granted, Sir, you have concluded to comply with what will no dout be the general call of your country in relation to the new government. You will permit me to say that it is indispensable you should lend yourself to its first operations. It is to little purpose to have *introduced* a system, if the weightiest influence is not given to its firm *establishment*, in the outset.

I remain with the greatest esteem
D Sir Yr. Obed & hum servant

A Hamilton

New York Aug 13. 1788

General Washington

TO HENRY LEE

"Light-Horse Harry" Lee had asked Hamilton, recently appointed Secretary of the Treasury, for private information on the probable future value of public securities.

My Dear Friend
I have received your letter of the 16th instant.

I am sure you are sincere when you say, you would not subject me to an impropriety. Nor do I know that there would be any in my answering your queries. But you remember the saying with regard to Caesar's Wife. I think the spirit of it applicable to every man concerned in the administration of the finances of a Country. With respect to the Conduct of such men, SUSPICION is ever eagle eyed, and the most innocent things are apt to be misinterpreted.

Be assured of the affection & friendship of

Yrs.

New York December 1st 1789   A Hamilton

H Lee Esqr

TO PHILIP HAMILTON

Philip Hamilton, just under ten, was at school at Trenton. Hamilton's resolve never to break a promise to a child accords with approved modern advice to parents.

Philadelphia
December 5 1791

I received with great pleasure My Dear Philip the letter which you wrote me last week. Your Mama and myself were very happy to learn that you are pleased with your situation and content to stay as long as shall be thought for your good. We hope and believe that nothing will happen to alter this disposition.

Your Master also informs me that you recited a lesson the first day you began, very much to his satisfaction. I expect every letter from him will give me a fresh proof of your progress. For I know that you can do a great deal, if you please, and I am sure you have too much spirit not to exert yourself, that you may make us every day more and more proud of you.

Your Mama has got an Ovid for you and is looking up your Mans introduction. If it cannot be found tomorrow another will be procured—and the books with the other articles she promised to send you will be forwarded in two or three days

You remember that I engaged to send for you next Saturday and I will do it unless you request me to put it off. For a promise must never be broken; and I never will make you one, which I will not fulfill as far as I am able. But it has occurred to me that the Christmas holidays are near at hand and I suppose your school will then break up for some days and give you an opportunity of coming to stay with us for a longer time than if you should come on Saturday. Will it not be best for you, therefore, to put off your journey till the holidays? But determine as you like best and let me know what will be most pleasing to you.

A good night to my darling son—

Adieu

A Hamilton

Master Philip A Hamilton

TO WILLIAM DUER

Hamilton was personally attached to Duer, who briefly had been Assistant Secretary of the Treasury. Duer's reckless speculation brought him to ruin and to jail. Hamilton helped obtain his temporary release from confinement.

My dear Duer: Philadelphia, March 14, 1792.

Your letter of the 11th got to hand this day. I am affected beyond measure at its contents, especially as it was too late to have any influence upon the event you were apprehensive of, Mr. Wolcott's instructions having gone off yesterday.

I trust, however, the alternative which they present to the attorney of the ———, and the discretion he will use in managing the affair, will enable you to avoid any pernicious *eclat*, if your affairs are otherwise retrievable.

Be this as it may, act with *fortitude* and *honor*. If you cannot reasonably hope for a favorable extrication, do not plunge deeper. Have the courage to make a full stop. Take all the care you can in the first place of institutions of public utility, and in the next of all fair creditors.

God bless you, and take care of you and your family. I have experienced all the bitterness of soul on your account which a warm

attachment can inspire. I will not now pain you with any wise remarks, though if you recover the present stroke, I shall take great
liberties with you. Assure yourself, in good and bad fortune, of my
sincere friendship and affection.

TO ONE OF THE CREDITORS
OF WILLIAM DUER

Dear Sir: August, 1793.

Poor *Duer* has now had a long and severe confinement, such as
would be adequate punishment for no trifling crime. I am well aware
of all the blame to which he is liable and do not mean to be his
apologist, though I believe he has been much the dupe of his own
imagination as others have been the victims of his projects. But
what then? He is a man—he is a man with whom we have both
been in habits of friendly intimacy. He is a man who, with a great
deal of good zeal, has in critical times rendered valuable services
to the country. He is a husband who has a most worthy and amiable
wife perishing with chagrin at his situation; your relation by blood,
mine by marriage. He is a father who has a number of fine children
destitute of the means of education and support, every way in need
of his future exertions.

These are titled to sympathy, which I shall be mistaken if you
do not feel. You are his creditor. Your example may influence
others. He wants permission, through a letter of license, to breathe
the air for five years. Your signature to the inclosed draft of one
will give me much pleasure.

CABINET PAPER
TO PRESIDENT WASHINGTON

President Washington, from Mount Vernon, had referred to the Secretary of the Treasury objections he had heard to the conduct of the
federal administration, particularly criticisms by George Mason of the

funding system. Hamilton introduced his detailed reply by the following spirited self-defense.

Sir   Philadelphia, Aug 18. 1792.

I am happy to be able, at length, to send you answers to the objections which were communicated in your letter of the 29th of July.

They have unavoidably been drawn in haste, too much so, to do perfect justice to the subject, and have been copied just as they flowed from my heart and pen, without revision or correction. You will observe that here and there some severity appears. I have not fortitude enough always to bear with calmness, calumnies, which necessarily include me, as a principal Agent in the measures censured, of the falsehood of which I have the most unqualified consciousness. I trust that I shall always be able to bear, as I ought, imputations of errors of Judgment; but I acknowledge that I cannot be intirely patient under charges, which impeach the integrity of my public motives or conduct. I feel, that I merit them *in no degree;* and expressions of indignation sometimes escape me, in spite of every effort to suppress them. I rely on your goodness for the proper allowances.

With high respect and the most affectionate attachment, I have the honor to be, Sir

Your most Obedient
                        & humble servant,
                                    Alexander Hamilton
The President of the United States

CONCERNING AARON BURR

The following are early letters pointing to the dangerous ambitions of Aaron Burr. Hamilton was similarly apprehensive of Burr for the next dozen years, and opposed Burr's career with results fatal to himself. Ironically, Hamilton later was hostile to John Adams, which redounded to the benefit of Jefferson.

Philadelphia September
21. 1792

Dear Sir

I take the liberty to inclose you the copy of a letter from a very respectable friend in New York. The contents surprised me, nor am I quite persuaded that the appearance of Mr. Burr on the stage is not a diversion in favour of Mr. Clinton.

Mr. Clinton's success I should think very unfortunate. I am not for trusting the Government too much in the hands of its enemies. But still Mr. C— is a man of property, and, in private life, as far as I know of probity. I fear the other Gentleman is unprincipled both as a public and private man. When the constitution was in deliberation, his conduct was equivocal; but its enemies, who I believe best understood him considered him as with them. In fact, I take it, he is for or against nothing, but as it suits his interest or ambition. He is determined, as I conceive, to make his way to be the head of the popular party and to climb per *fas et nefas* to the highest honors of the State; and as much higher as circumstances may permit. Embarrassed, as I understand, in his circumstances, with an extravagant family, bold enterprising and intriguing, I am mistaken, if it be not his object to play the game of confusion, and I feel it a religious duty to oppose his career.

I have hitherto scrupulously refrained from interference in elections. But the occasion is in my opinion of sufficient importance to warrant in this instance a departure from that rule. I therefore commit my opinion to you without scruple, but in perfect confidence. I pledge my character for discernment that it is incumbent upon every good man to resist the present design.

TO GENERAL CHARLES C. PINCKNEY

Philadelphia, Oct. 10th 1792

My Dear Sir:

I duly received your letter of the 6th September; and have sent an extract of it to Mr. Church for the explanation which is necessary.

I feel myself truly obliged by your friendly allusion to my unpleasant situation, and for the consolation you are so kind as to offer me. The esteem of the discerning and virtuous must always support a mind properly formed under the pressure of malevolence and envy. I will not pretend that I am insensible to the persecution which I experience; but it may be relied upon that I shall desert no post which I ought to endeavour to maintain, so long as my own reputation or the public good may render perseverance necessary or proper. When it is not requisite either to the one or the other my friends will excuse me, if I recollect that I have a growing and hitherto too much neglected family. It is to be lamented that so strong a spirit of faction and innovation prevails at the present moment in a great part of the Country. The thing is alarming enough to call for the attention of every friend to Government. Let me not be thought to travel out of my sphere if I observe that a particular attention to the election for the next Congress is dictated by the vigorous and general effort which is making by factious men to introduce every where and in every department persons unfriendly to the measures, if not the constitution, of the National Government. Either Governor Clinton, or Mr. Burr of New York, both decidedly of the description of persons I have mentioned, is to be run in this quarter as Vice-President in opposition to Mr. Adams. The former has been invariably the enemy of national principles. The latter has no other principles than *to mount, at all events*, to the first honors of the State & to as much more as circumstances will permit; a man in private life not unblemished. It will be a real misfortune to the Government if either of them should prevail. Tis suspected by some that the plan is only to divide the votes of the Northern & the Middle States, to let in Mr. Jefferson by the votes of the South. I will not scruple to say to you in confidence that this also would be a serious misfortune to the Government. That gentleman whom I once *very much esteemed*, but who does not permit me to retain that sentiment for him, is certainly a man of sublimated and paradoxical imagination, entertaining and propagating notions inconsistent with dignified and orderly Government. Mr. Adams whatever objections may lie against some of his theoretic opinions is a firm honest independent politician. Some valuable characters are about to be lost to the House of Representatives of their own choice. I feared once that this would be the case with Mr. Smith, of your state; but I believe his present intention is rather to continue to serve. I trust there can be no doubt of his success and I wish means to be used to determine his acquiescence. He is truly an excellent member—a ready clear speaker of a sound analytic head and the justest views. I know no man whose loss from the House would be more severely felt by the good cause. The delicacy of these observations from me will of course occur to you. I make them without reserve confiding equally in your friendship and prudence. Accept the assurances of the cordial esteem & regard with which I have the honor to remain.

D Sir

Yr. Obedient Servant

Alex Hamilton

Charles Cotsworth Pinckney Esq.

TO NICHOLAS GOUVERNEUR

The following shows how Hamilton scrupulously upheld the good name of the legal profession.

Sir

Mr Bremar last evening delivered me your Letter inclosing a Copy of your Correspondence with Mr ——

In a personal Altercation between two Gentlemen where their passions have evidently become pretty warmly engaged, and for both whom I always had Esteem, I should not be willing to give my Opinion on the conduct of one of them, especially when the appeal was not made to me by both. On this head I shall only take the

Liberty to say, that I would not advise *publication* which has always a disagreeable appearance, and seldom turns out to the Advantage of either party.

In another respect I feel myself painfully situated. Having received favourable impressions of your Character, I am sorry to observe any thing to have come from you which I am obliged to consider as exceptionable. Your second Letter to Mr —— contains a *general* and of Course an unjustifiable reflection on the profession to which I belong and of a Nature to put it out of my power to attempt to render you any service in the line of that profession. I readily believe you did not attend to the full force of the Expression, when you tell Mr —— "[the] *Attorney likes*" to make the most of his bill of Costs: but it contains in it an insinuation which cannot be pleasing to any man in the Profession and which must oblige anyone that has proper delicacy to decline the business of one who professedly entertains Such an Idea of the Conduct of his profession.

I make allowances for your feelings when you wrote that Letter, and am therefore reluctantly drawn into these Observations.

I remain with Esteem

Sir

Your Obedient sevt.

A Hamilton

FIRST DRAFT OF A DEMAND

Anything connecting Hamilton with a duel has special interest, since he was to die in the most famous duel in American history. The letter below gives Hamilton's complaints against Commodore James Nicholson, growing out of a political dispute in 1795. Later Hamilton revised this letter to make it shorter and less offensive. Nicholson was the father-in-law of Gallatin. The quarrel was composed without a fight.

Mr Hamilton declares & would repeat that when he interposed in the altercation between Mr Nicholson & Mr Hoffman what he said was addressed to both & was purely intended without offence to either to prevent the continuance of a controversy which might lead to disturbance & riot

Mr Nicholson replied very harshly to Mr Hamilton that he was not the man to prevent his quarreling called him an Abettor of Tories and used some other harsh expressions which are forgotten.

Mr Hamilton replied that that was not a place for altercation & Mr Nicholson & he would discuss it upon a more fit occasion

Mr Nicholson replied he Mr Hamilton would not pursue the affair for he had declined an interview upon a former occasion

Mr Hamilton replied that no man could affirm that with truth & that he pledged himself to convince Mr Nicholson of his mistake

Here then was clearly a violent offence without provocation

If Mr Nicholson is disposed to accommodation justace & propriety require that he should say

That the subject of offence to Mr Hamilton was the effect of misapprehension & temporary passion—that he does not entertain the opinion which his declaration would seem to imply and that he regrets the pain which it must have given to Mr Hamilton

TO GENERAL GEORGE WASHINGTON

After France, locked in war with England, had trespassed on our rights as neutral carrier, and had insulted our emissaries, America prepared for war against her. Washington, called to chief command, designated Hamilton next in rank, which gave him, practically, responsibility for organizing the defense. President Adams agreed only under Washington's compulsion. Knox resigned in disgust. Hamilton exaggerated the crisis, put himself forward too eagerly.

Philadelphia, July 29, 1798.

My dear Sir:

Your letter of the 14th instant did not reach me till after the appointments mentioned in it were made.

I see clearly in what has been done a new mark of your confidence, which I value as I ought to do.

With regard to the delicate subject of the relative rank of the major-generals, it is very natural for me to be a partial judge, and it is not very easy for me to speak upon it. If I know myself, however, this, at least, I may say, that, were I convinced of injustice being done to others in my favor, I should not hesitate even to volunteer a correction of it, as far as my consent would avail. But in a case like this, am I not to take the opinion of others as my guide? If I am, the conclusion is that the gentlemen concerned ought to acquiesce. It is a fact of which there is a flood of evidence that a great majority of leading Federal men were of opinion that in the event of your declining the command of the army, it ought to devolve upon me, and that in case of your acceptance, which everybody ardently desired, the place of second in command ought to be mine.

It is not for me to examine the justness of this opinion. The illusions of self-love might be expected too easily to give it credit with me. But finding it to exist, am I at liberty to seek to postpone myself to others, in whose hands, according to that opinion, the public interests would be less well confided? Such are the reflections which would have determined me to let the business take its course.

My own opinion, at the same time, is, that of the two gentlemen postponed to me, the cause of complaint, if any, applies emphatically to General Knox. His rank in the army was much higher than that either of Pinckney or myself. Pinckney's pretensions on the score of real service are not extensive; those of Knox are far greater. Pinckney has, no doubt, studied tactics with great care and assiduity, but it is not presumable that he is as well versed in the tactics of a general as *Knox*.

Pinckney's rank at the close of the war was only nominally greater than mine; it was, indeed, of more ancient date. But when, in the year 1777, the regiments of artillery were multiplied, I had good reason to expect that the command of one of them would have fallen to me, had I not changed my situation. And this, in all probability, would have led further. I am aware, at the same time, that there were accidental impediments to Pinckney's progress in preferment, but an accurate comparison would, I imagine, show that, on the score of rank merely, the claim of superiority on his part is not strongly marked. As to military *service*, I venture to believe that the general understanding of the late army would allow a considerable balance to me.

As to civil services since the war, I am extremely mistaken if, in the minds of Federal men, there is any comparison between us. The circumstances of the moment, it is true, give him a certain *eclat*, but judicious men reduce the merit to the two points of judicious *forbearance* and the *firmness* not to sacrifice his country by base compliances. In all this, it is very far from my inclination to detract from General Pinckney. I have a sincere regard for him, and hold him in high estimation. At the same time, endeavoring to view the matter with all the impartiality which my situation permits, I must conclude that General Pinckney, on a fair estimate of all circumstances, ought to be well satisfied with the arrangement.

After saying this much, I will add that regard to the public interest is ever predominant with me; that if the gentlemen concerned are dissatisfied, and the service likely to suffer by the preference given to me, I stand ready to submit our relative pretensions to an impartial decision, and to waive the preference. It shall *never* be said, with any color of truth, that my ambition or interest has stood in the way of the public good.

Thus, sir, have I opened my heart to you with as little reserve as to myself, willing, rather, that its weakness should appear than that I should be deficient in frankness. I will only add that I do not think it necessary to make public beforehand the ultimate intentions I have now disclosed.

It is possible the difficulties anticipated may not arise. But, my dear sir, there is a matter of far greater moment than all this, which I must do violence to my friendship by stating to you, but of which it is essential you should be apprised. It is that my friend McHenry is wholly insufficient for his place, with the additional misfortune of not having himself the least suspicion of the fact. This generally will not surprise you, when you take into view the large scale upon which he is now to act. But you perhaps may not be aware of the whole extent of the insufficiency. It is so great as to leave no probability that the business of the War Department can make any tolerable progress in his hands. This has been long observed, and has been more than once mentioned to the President by members of Congress.

He is not insensible, I believe, that the execution of the department does not produce the expected results; but the case is of course delicate and embarrassing.

My real friendship for McHenry, concurring with my zeal for the service, predisposed me to aid him in all that he could properly throw upon me, and I thought that he would have been glad, in the organization of the army, and in the conduct of the recruiting service, to make me useful to him. With this view, I came to this city, and I previously opened the way as far as I could with the least decency. But the idea has thus far been very partially embraced, and to-morrow or next day I shall return to New York, without much fruit of my journey. I mention this purely to apprise you of the course of things, and the probable results.

It is to be regretted that the supposition of cooperation between the Secretary of War and the Principal military officers will unavoidably throw upon the latter a part of the blame which the ill success of the operations of the War Department may be expected to produce. Thus you perceive, sir, your perplexities are begun.

P.S.—Since writing the above, I have concluded to write a letter, of which the enclosed is the copy. This effort to save a man I value, and promote the service, has, under the circumstances, cost some thing to my delicacy.

Mr. Harper, of the House of Representatives, is desirous of being in your family. He is a man of very *considerable talents* and has the temper of a soldier. The shade of his useful qualities is *vanity*, but I think the good much outweighs the ill. Pardon this liberty in a point so delicate.

New York, Aug. 1, 1798.

The above was written at Philadelphia, but a very pressing call to this place, added to occupation there, prevented my being able to copy and forward it till now.

Give me leave to suggest the expediency of your asking of McHenry a statement of all the military supplies, cannon, arms, etc., etc., which are already provided and in execution for augmenting the quantity. This will give you necessary information and prompt to exertion.

TO OLIVER WOLCOTT

When Jefferson and Burr received the same number of votes for the presidency the election was thrown into the House of Representatives. Hamilton exerted himself with leading Federalists to defeat Burr, whom he distrusted as man and politician, and to throw their favor to Jefferson, for whom, in spite of deep differences of principle, Hamilton had elements of respect.

[December] 1800

Your last letter, My Dear Sir, has given me great pain; not only because it informed me that the opinion in favour of Mr. Burr was increasing among the Federalists, but because it also told me that Mr. Sedgwick was one of its partisans. I have a letter from this Gentleman, in which he expresses decidedly his preference of Mr. Jefferson. I hope you have been mistaken and that it is not possible for him to have been guilty of so great duplicity.

There is no circumstance which has occurred in the course of our political affairs that has given me so much pain as the idea that Mr. Burr might be elevated to the Presidency by the means of the Federalists. I am of opinion that this party has hitherto solid claims of merit with the public and so long as it does nothing to forfeit its title to confidence I shall continue to hope that our misfortunes are temporary and that the party will erelong emerge from its depression. But if it shall act a foolish or unworthy part in any capital instance, I shall then despair.

Such without doubt will be the part it will act, if it shall seriously attempt to support Mr. Burr, in opposition to Mr. Jefferson. If it fails, as after all is not improbable, it will have riveted the animosity of that person, will have destroyed or weakened the motives to moderation which he must at present feel and it will expose them to the disgrace of a defeat in an attempt to elevate to the first place in the Government one of the worst men in the community.

If it succeeds it will have done nothing more nor less than place in that station a man who will possess the boldness and daring necessary to give success to the Jacobin system instead of one who for want of that quality will be less fitted to promote it.

Let it not be imagined that Mr. Burr can be won to the Federal Views. It is a vain hope. Stronger ties, and stronger inducements than they can offer, will impel him in a different direction. His ambition will not be content with these objects which virtuous men of either party will allot to it, and his situation and his habits will oblige him to have recourse to corrupt expedients, from which he will be restrained by no moral Scruples. To accomplish his ends he must lean upon unprincipled men and will continue to adhere to the myrmidons who have hitherto seconded him. To these he will no doubt add able rogues of the Federal party; but he will employ the rogues of all parties to overrule the good men of all parties, and to prosecute projects which wise men of every description will disapprove.

These things are to be inferred with moral certainty from the character of the man. Every step in his career proves that he has formed himself upon the model of *Catiline*, and he is too cold-blooded and too determined a conspirator ever to change his plan. . . .

.   .   .   .

If Jefferson is President the whole responsibility of bad measures will rest with the Antifederalists. If Burr is made so by the Federalists the whole responsibility will rest with them. The other party will say to the People, We intended him only for vice-President. Here he might have done very well or been at least harmless. But the Federalists[,] to disappoint us and a majority of you[,] took advantage of a momentary superiority to put him in the first place. He is therefore their President and they must answer for all the Evils of his bad conduct. And the People will believe them.

Will any reasonable calculation on the part of the Federalists uphold the policy of assuming so great a responsibility in the support of so unpromising a character? The negative is so manifest that had I not been assured of the contrary I should have thought it impossible that assent to it would have been attended with a moment's hesitation.

Alas! when will men consult their reason rather than their passions? Whatever they may imagine the desire of mortifying the adverse party must be the chief spring of the disposition to prefer Mr. Burr. This disposition reminds me of the conduct of the Dutch moneyed men who from hatred of the old Aristocracy favoured the admission of the French into Holland to overturn every thing.

Adieu to the Federal Troy, if they once introduce this Grecian Horse into their Citadel.

Trust me my Dear friend, you cannot render a greater service to your country than to resist this project. Far better will it be to endeavour to obtain from Jefferson assurances on some cardinal points—1 The preservation of the actual Fiscal System 2 Adherence to the Neutral plan. 3 The preservation & gradual increase of the Navy 4 The continuance of our friends in the offices they fill except in the great departments in which he ought to be left free.

Adieu My Dr. Sr

Yrs ever

A Hamilton

O Wolcott esq

TO DOCTOR RUSH

The tragic death of young Philip Hamilton brought more sorrows than were included in his father's response to the condolences of Rush. Angelica, next to Philip in age, was so distressed that her mind was permanently affected.

Dr. Sir   New York Feby 12. 1802
   I felt all the wieght of the obligation which I owed to you and to your amiable family for the tender concern they manifested in an event beyond comparison the most afflecting of my life. But I was obliged to wait for a moment of greater calm to express my sense of the kindness.

   My loss is indeed great. The brightest as well as the eldest hope of my family has been taken from me. You estimated him rightly. He was truly a fine youth. But why should I repine? It was the will of heaven: and he is now out of the reach of the seductions and calamities of a world, full of folly full of vice, full of danger— of least value in proportion as it is best known. I firmly trust, also, that he has safely reached the haven of eternal repose and felicity.

   You will easely conscieve that every memorial of the goodness of his heart must be precious to me. You allude to one recorded in a letter to your son. If no special reasons forbid it, I should be very glad to have a copy of that letter.

   Mrs. Hamilton who has drunk deeply of the cup of sorrow joins me in affectionate thanks to Mrs. Rush and yourself. Our wishes for your happiness will be unceasing.
             Very sincerely & cordially
                       Yrs. A. Hamilton

H to
To Doctr. Rush
1802. Feby 12th

TO ELIZABETH HAMILTON

The affection with which Hamilton planned his country home (in the vicinity of the present 142d Street and Tenth Avenue) appears in the following. The house was commenced in 1800, and is still standing, though in a different location.

Claverack, Oct 14, 1803

My Dear Eliza

I arrived here this day, in about as good health as I left home though somewhat fatigued.

There are some things necessary to be done which I omitted mentioning to you. I wish the carpenters to make and insert two chimnies for ventilating the Ice-House, each about two feet square and four feet long half above and half below the ground—to have a cap on the top sloping down wards so that the rain may not easily enter. The aperture for letting in and out the air to be about a foot and a half square in the side immediately below the cap (see *figure* on the other side).

Let a separate compost bed be formed near the present one; to consist of 3 barrels full of *clay* which I bought[,] barrels of *block Mould* 2 waggon loads of the best clay on the Hill opposite the *Quakers place* this side of Mr. Verplanks (the Gardener must go for it himself) and one waggon load of pure cow-dung. Let these be well and repeatedly mixed together to be made use of hereafter for the vines.

I hope the apple trees will have been planted so as to profit by this moderate and wet weather. If not done, Let *Tough* be reminded that a temporary fence is to be put up along the declivity of the Hill from the King's bridge road to the opposite wood so as to prevent the cattle injuring the young trees. The fence near the entrance to the *Helicon spring* ought for the same reason to be attended to. The materials of the fence taken down in making the Kitchen Garden & some rubbish which may be picked up will answer.

Remember that the piazzas are also to be caulked & that additional accommodations for the pidgeons are to be made.

You see I do not forget the Grange. No[,] that I do not; nor any-one that inhabits it. Accept yourself my tenderest affection. Give my love to your children & remember me to Cornelia. Adieu my darling.

AH

Mrs. H

HAMILTON'S ASSETS AND DEBTS

The following statement of Hamilton's financial position and prospects was probably written not earlier than 1802 and perhaps as late as 1804 when his duel with Burr was in the wind. It shows his nice sense of obligation to creditors.

Herewith is a general statement of my pecuniary affairs, in which there can be no material error.

The result is that calculating my property at what it stands me in, I am now worth about £10,000, and that estimating according to what my lands are now selling for and are likely to fetch, the surplus beyond my debts may fairly be stated at nearly double that sum; yet I am pained to be obliged to entertain doubts, whether, if an accident should happen to me, by which the sales of my property should come to be forced, it would even be sufficient to pay my debts. In a situation like this, it is perhaps due to my reputation to explain why I have made so considerable an establishment in the country. This explanation shall be submitted.

To men who have been so much harassed in the base world as myself, it is natural to look forward to a comfortable retirement, in the sequel of life, as a principal desideratum. This desire I have felt in the strongest manner, and to prepare for it has latterly been a favorite object. I thought I might not only expect to accomplish the object, but might reasonably aim at it and pursue the prepara-tory measures, from the following considerations:

It has been for some time past pretty well ascertained to my mind, that the emoluments of my profession would prove equal to the maintenance of my family and the gradual discharge of my debts, within a period to the end of which my faculties for business might be expected to extend in full energy. I think myself warranted to estimate the annual product of those emoluments at twelve thousand dollars at the least. My expenses while the first improvements of my country establishment were going on have been great, but they would this summer and fall reach the point at which, it is my intention they should stop, at least till I should be better able than at present to add to them; and after a fair examination founded upon an actual account of my expenditure, I am persuaded that a plan I have contemplated for the next and succeeding years would bring my expenses of every kind within the compass of four thousand dollars yearly, exclusive of the interest of my country establishment. To this limit I have been resolved to reduce them, even though it should be necessary to lease that establishment for a few years. In the meantime, my lands now in a course of sale and settlement would accelerate the extinguishment of my debts, and in the end leave me a handsome clear property. It was also allowable for me to take into view collaterally the expectations of my wife: which have been of late partly realized. She is now entitled to a property of between 2,000 and 3,000 pounds (as I compute), by descent from her mother, and her father is understood to possess a large estate. I feel all the delicacy of this allusion, but the occasion, I trust, will plead my excuses, and that venerable father, I am sure, will pardon. He knows well all the nicety of my past conduct.

Viewing the matter in these different aspects, I trust the opinion of candid men will be that there has been no impropriety in my conduct, especially when it is taken into the calculation, that my country establishment, though costly, promises, by the progressive rise of property on this island and the felicity of its situation, to become more and more valuable. My chief apology is to those friends who have from mere kindness endorsed my paper discounted at the banks. On mature reflection I have thought it justifiable to secure them in preference to other creditors, lest perchance there should be a deficit. Yet, while this may save them from eventual loss, it will not exempt them from present inconvenience. As to this I can only throw myself upon their kindness and entreat the indulgence of the banks for them. Perhaps the request may be supposed entitled to some regard. In the event which would bring this paper to the public eye, one thing at least would be put beyond doubt. This is that my public labors have amounted to an absolute sacrifice of the interests of my family, and that in all pecuniary concerns the delicacy no less than the probity of conduct in public stations has been such as to defy even the shadow of a question.

Indeed, I have not enjoyed the ordinary advantages incident to my military services. Being a member of Congress while the question of the commutation of the half pay of the army for a sum in gross was in debate, delicacy and a desire to be useful to the army by removing the idea of my having an interest in the question, induced me to write to the Secretary of War and relinquish my claim to half pay, which or the equivalent I have never received. Neither have I even applied for the lands allowed by the United States to officers of my rank. Nor did I ever obtain from this State the allowance of lands made to officers of similar rank. It is true that having served through the latter periods of the war on the general staff of the United States and not in the line of this State, I could not claim the allowance as a matter of course; but having before the war resided in this State, and having entered the military career at the head of a company of artillery raised for the particular defence of this State, I had better pretensions to the allowance than others to whom it was actually made, yet it has not been extended to me.

A.H.

HAMILTON'S MOTIVES IN MEETING BURR

Hamilton's explanation of why he felt compelled to accept Burr's challenge to a duel speaks for itself. It seems established from various testimony that Hamilton held to his resolve not to discharge his pistol at Burr. The first of his farewell letters to his wife was written a week in advance of the fatal encounter. The second, penned the night before the duel, asks her kindness to his cousin, who had befriended him in his boyhood. She carried out his wishes to the best of her ability, and Hamilton's old friend and patron, Elias Boudinot, also aided Ann Mitchell generously.

On my expected interview with Col. Burr, I think it proper to make some remarks explanatory of my conduct, motives, and views. I was certainly desirous of avoiding this interview for the most cogent reasons.

1. My religious and moral principles are strongly opposed to the practice of duelling, and it would ever give me pain to be obliged to shed the blood of a fellow creature in a private combat forbidden by the laws.

2. My wife and children are extremely dear to me, and my life is of the utmost importance to them, in various views.

3. I feel a sense of obligation towards my creditors; who in case of accident to me, by the forced sale of my property, may be in some degree sufferers. I did not think myself at liberty as a man of probity, lightly to expose them to this hazard.

4. I am conscious of no *illwill* to Col. Burr, distinct from political opposition, which, as I trust, has proceeded from pure and upright motives.

Lastly, I shall hazard much and can possibly gain nothing by the issue of the interview.

But it was, as I conceive, impossible for me to avoid it. There were *intrinsic* difficulties in the thing, and *artificial* embarrassments, from the manner of proceeding on the part of Col. Burr.

Intrinsic, because it is not to be denied that my animadversions on the political principles, character, and views of Col. Burr have been extremely severe; and on different occasions I, in common with many others have made very unfavorable criticisms on particular instances of the private conduct of this gentleman. In proportion as these impressions were entertained with sincerity, and uttered with motives and for purposes which might appear to me commendable, would be the difficulty (until they could be removed by evidence of their being erroneous,) of explanation or apology. The disavowal required of me by Col. Burr, in a general and indefinite form, was out of my power, if it had really been proper for me to submit to be so questioned; but I was sincerely of opinion that this could not be, and in this opinion, I was confirmed by that of a very moderate and judicious friend whom I consulted. Besides that, Col. Burr appeared to me to assume, in the first instance, a tone unnecessarily peremptory and menacing, and in the second, positively offensive. Yet I wished, as far as might be practicable, to leave a door open to accommodation. This, I think, will be inferred from the written communication made by me and by my direction, and would be confirmed by the conversations between Mr. Van Ness and myself, which arose out of the subject. I am not sure whether, under all the circumstances, I did not go further in the attempt to accommodate than a punctilious delicacy will justify. If so, I hope the motives I have stated will excuse me. It is not my design, by what I have said, to affix any odium on the conduct of Col. Burr, in this case. He doubtless has heard of animadversions of mine which bore very hard upon him; and it is probable that as usual they were accompanied with some falsehoods. He may have supposed himself under a necessity of acting as he has done. I hope the grounds of his proceeding have been such as ought to satisfy his own conscience. I trust, at the same time, that the world will do me the justice to believe that I have not censured him on light grounds, nor from unworthy inducements. I certainly have had strong reasons for what I have said, though it is possible that in some particulars I may have been influenced by misconstruction or misinformation. It is also my ardent wish that I may have been more mistaken than I think I have been and that he, by his future conduct, may show himself worthy of all confidence and esteem, and prove an ornament and a blessing to the country. As well because it is possible that I may have injured Col. Burr, however convinced myself that my opinions and declarations have been well founded, as from my general principles and temper in relation to similar affairs, I have resolved, if our interview is conducted in the usual manner, and it pleases God to give me the opportunity, to *reserve* and *throw away* my first fire, and I *have thoughts* even of *reserving* my second fire, and thus giving a double opportunity to Col. Burr to pause and reflect. It is not, however, my intention to enter into any explanations on the ground. Apology from principle, I hope, rather than pride, is out of the question. To those who, with me, abhorring the practice of duelling, may think that I ought on no account to have added to the number of bad examples, I answer, that my *relative* situation, as well in public as private, enforcing all the considerations which constitute what men of the world denominate honour, imposed on me (as I thought) a peculiar necessity not to decline the call. The ability to be in future useful, whether in resisting mischief or effecting good, in those crises of our public affairs which seem likely to happen, would probably be inseparable from a conformity with public prejudice in this particular.

TO ELIZABETH HAMILTON

This letter, my very dear Eliza, will not be delivered to you, unless I shall first have terminated my earthly career; to begin, as I humbly hope from redeeming grace and divine mercy, a happy immortality.

If it had been possible for me to have avoided the interview, my love for you and my precious children would have been alone a decisive motive. But it was not possible, without sacrifices which would have rendered me unworthy of your esteem. I need not tell you of the pangs I feel, from the idea of quitting you and exposing you to the anguish which I know you would feel. Nor could I dwell on the topic lest it should unman me.

The consolations of Religion, my beloved, can alone support you; and these you have a right to enjoy. Fly to the bosom of your God and be comforted. With my last idea, I shall cherish the sweet hope of meeting you in a better world. Adieu best of wives and best of women. Embrace all my Darling Children for me.

Ever yours

AH

July 4. 1804

Mrs. Hamilton

My Beloved Eliza:

    Mrs. Mitchel is the person in the world to whom as a friend I am under the greatest obligation. I have not hitherto done my duty to her. But resolved to repair my omission to her as much as possible, I have encouraged her to come to this country, and intended, if it shall be in my power to render the Evening of her days comfortable. But if it shall please God to put this out of my power, and to inable you hereafter to be of service to her, I entreat you to do it and to treat her with the tenderness of a sister. This is my second letter. The scruples of a Christian have determined me to expose my own life to any extent rather than subject myself to the guilt of taking the life of another. This must increase my hazards and redoubles my pangs for you. But you had rather I should die innocent than live guilty. Heaven can preserve me and I humbly hope will; but, in the contrary event, I charge you to remember that you are a Christian. God's will be done! The will of a merciful God must be good. Once more,

Adieu, my darling, darling wife

AH

Tuesday Even'g   10 ocl

Mrs. Hamilton